A HISTORY OF ENGLISH LITERATURE

Volume I

(In Four Volumes)

by

Chen Jia

The Commercial Press

1988 · Beijing

YĪNG GUÓ WÉN XUÉ SHǏ

英 国 文 学 史

第 一 册

陈 嘉 著

商 务 印 书 馆 出 版

（北京王府井大街 36 号）

新 华 书 店 北 京 发 行 所 发 行

北京第二新华印刷厂印刷

ISBN 7-100-00192-7/G·58

1982 年 7 月第 1 版　　　　开本 850×1168 1/32

1988 年 2 月北京第 5 次印刷　　字数 318 千

印数 10,100 册　　　　　　印张 10 5/8

定价: 1.65 元

FOREWORD

This is an attempt to write a history of English literature admittedly with an innovative approach. The traditional as well as the more modern views in the West on literary movements, schools, traditions and influences in the field of English literature and on individual English authors and their major and minor works are here given due respect and serious consideration, but with the reservation sometimes to differ and occasionally to introduce new and totally contrary judgments from the viewpoint of historical materialism — i.e., the writers and their writings are to be given their proper places in each case in accordance with the roles, healthful or otherwise, that they play in the progress of history, social and literary. Of course, whether or how far have I succeeded in these pages in living up to the theory advanced above awaits judgment from my readers.

This history is written primarily for Chinese readers, in particular for Chinese college students majoring in English language and literature, with the aim to give them a historical survey of English literature from its earliest beginnings down to the 20th century. As many college students in China today are being introduced for the first time to English literature in any systematic way, biographical sketches of the major writers and rather detailed resumés of their major works are generally provided in this history, before I enter into any serious discussions on the authors and their writings.

A companion-book providing students with selections from representative works of representative English authors, arranged chronologically and accompanied with introductory remarks and notes, is expected to appear at the same time as this history. It is hoped that the two books together, this history and "Selected Readings in

English Literature", will give the students a rudimentary knowledge of English literature in its historical development.

In view of the vastly different levels of proficiency in the English language among English majors in Chinese colleges and universities today, a shorter history than this, written in simpler language, seems also necessary for the present. Such a book is now being prepared.

I wish to express my gratitude here to all my friends and colleagues as well as my former students who have given me their valuable suggestions in the course of writing this book. My indebtedness is due particularly to the participants at a conference held prior to the completion of the book, and they include Professors Li Funing and Yang Zhouhan (both from Beijing University), Wu Jingrong (Beijing Institute of Foreign Languages), Dai Liuling (Zhongshan University), Zhang Junchuan (Hangzhou University), Zhang Jian (Shandong University), Huang Hongxu (Hobei Normal University), Associate and Assistant Professors Sun Zhu (Fudan University), Liu Yulin (Shanghai Institute of Foreign Languages), Long Wenpei (Fudan University), Liu Bingshan (Honan Normal University), Luo Yiyun (Sichuan University), Xie Chulan (Nanjing University), Yang Renjing (Nanjing University), and last not least, Messrs. Zhu Yuan (editor, the Commercial Press), Liu Zucai and Xu Baofa (both from the Ministry of Education), as well as my two graduate students Liu Haiping and Wang Xisu. I am grateful to them all for their invaluable suggestions and comments. Finally I want to thank the working personnel at the Commercial Press who are directly responsible for the publication of this book.

Chen Jia

Contents

Chapter I

ENGLISH LITERATURE OF THE ANGLO-SAXON PERIOD

Chapter II

ENGLISH LITERATURE OF THE LATE MIDDLE AGES

Chapter III
ENGLISH LITERATURE OF
THE RENAISSANCE

Chapter IV
ENGLISH LITERATURE DURING THE ENGLISH BOURGEOIS REVOLUTION AND THE RESTORATION

Chapter I

ENGLISH LITERATURE OF THE ANGLO-SAXON PERIOD

1. The Historical Background.

Before the coming of the Anglo-Saxons, the Celtic tribes lived in what is now Britain. In the middle of the first century B.C., Roman troops led by Julius Caesar invaded Britain, then Claudius conquered it in A.D. 43 and Britain became a Roman province till the beginning of the fifth century. During their rule the Romans built roads, walls, garrisons, villas, etc., and the Celts became either slaves or unfree cultivators of the land. Then, in early 5th century, as the Germanic races attacked and overran the Roman Empire, the Roman garrisons in Britain withdrew.

Not long after that, in the mid-5th century, the tribes of Angles, Saxons and Jutes (later known simply as Anglo-Saxons) migrated to England from the European Continent, or more specifically from western Denmark and the northwest coast of Germany. They settled down there and soon ruled over the whole of England, enslaving some of the native Celts while driving the others to the hills north and west, to Wales and Scotland and even Ireland across the sea. Thus began the Anglo-Saxon period in English history.

While still on the Continent, the Anglo-Saxons were in the later stages of tribal society. Their common occupation was agriculture, with a small number of them already set apart as professional soldiers or as hereditary military leaders. Some of these leaders gradually became thanes or the nobility and a few of them rose to be chieftains or even kings. Settlement in Britain hastened the disintegration of tribalism as the tribal chieftains and thanes had the possession of large tracts of land and grew in wealth and power while the free farmers became more and more dependent economically.

By the 7th century, seven kingdoms of fairly large territories emerged out of more numerous smaller kingdoms and there were wars among them. Of the seven Mercia and then Northumberland in the north flourished particularly in wealth and culture in the 7th and 8th centuries, and Wessex in the south became a more important centre of military and political power and assumed supremacy in culture and learning in the 9th and 10th centuries. Beginning from late 8th century the Danes came to invade England and for more than a century they made intermittent raids on the eastern coast of Britain and occupied for fairly long periods of time large areas of northeastern England. In late 9th century King Alfred the Great (A.D. 849 - 901?) of the Kingdom of Wessex successfully led the English people in a protracted war against the invading Danes who were threatening to overrun the whole country. The invaders were repulsed and gradually all the kingdoms in England were united into one.

In early 11th century the Danes again came to invade England and under Canute they conquered and ruled over all England for a quarter of a century (A.D. 1017 – 1042). Then, following the expulsion of the Danes the Normans from Normandy in northern France came to invade England in 1066, and under the leadership of William the Duke of Normandy who claimed the succession to the English throne they succeeded in defeating the English troops and conquering the whole of England. The "Norman Conquest" marked the end of the Anglo-Saxon period.

In late Saxon England feudalism assumed definite shape, with the king at the top, then the earls and the thanes, then the freemen and last the serfs. Agriculture developed and trade expanded. Towns came into existence and wealth became more concentrated. With the Norman Conquest feudalism underwent further development.

The Anglo-Saxons were heathen upon their first arrival in England. In A.D. 597 the first missionaries led by St. Augustine came to England from Rome and converted King Ethelbert of Kent, and

2

within a century all England was Christianized. Churches were built and the monks were among the most learned in the country. The heathen mythology was gradually replaced by the Christian religion, but heathen concepts of nature and the supernatural persisted for a considerable period of time and often were curiously mixed with Christian views and expressions. This phenomenon found its expression not infrequently in literary works of the Anglo-Saxon period.

2. "Beowulf" the National Epic of the Anglo-Saxons.

The earliest poetry of the Anglo-Saxons, like that of many other peoples, originated from the collective efforts of the people, usually while they were working or resting from their labours. Then these stories based on history or legend or contemporaneous events would be narrated orally and often sung, during festivities and other occasions, chiefly for entertainment. Some of the more interesting of these narratives would pass from mouth to mouth, from generation to generation, and as they were told by different singers at different times, additions or deletions were introduced in the successive rehandlings of the oral tradition of each epic.

With the disintegration of tribal society and the appearance of class divisions, professional narrators or singers of these popular stories emerged. They were known as "scops" or "gleemen" among the Anglo-Saxons, the former being poet-singers who sang poetic tales of their own making while the latter mere retellers of epics already in circulation. At first these "scops" and "gleemen" also served as priests giving spells or citing incantations on various solemn occasions but later they became simply wandering minstrels travelling extensively from one chieftain's court to that of another, providing entertainment with their singing. Two of the earliest Anglo-Saxon lyrics extant, "Widsith" (probably of the 7th century) and "Deor's Lament" (probably of the 8th century), are good literary specimens that illustrate the life and social position of the later "scops" or "gleemen".

Because these popular narratives of the Anglo-Saxons in the earliest times existed originally in oral tradition and few of them seemed to have been handed down in written form, "Beowulf" is possibly the only important single poem of this kind preserved to this day more or less in its entirety and has generally been considered the most monumental work in English poetry of the Anglo-Saxon period.

"Beowulf" probably existed in its oral form as early as the 6th century and was written down in the 7th or 8th century, though the manuscript of the poem now extant dated back to the 10th century. It contains 3183 lines of alliterative verse, being the longest of the early Anglo-Saxon poems preserved. The story in the epic is based on part-historical, part-legendary material brought over to England by the Anglo-Saxons from their original homes on the European Continent. So Beowulf the hero of the poem and his adventures are placed in Denmark and southern Sweden rather than in England.

The poem opens with a brief account of the line of Danish kings down to Hrothgar, Beowulf's kinsman who builds a splendid hall named Heorot to entertain his followers (lines 1 – 100 in the poem). A monster by the name of Grendel frequently comes to the hall at night and at one time devours as many as thirty warriors sleeping there, so that the hall is deserted after dark (lines 101 – 193). The news of Grendel's ravages finally reaches southern Sweden, where Beowulf, nephew to King Hygelac of the Geats and a man of great strength, hears of it and sails with fourteen companions to lend help to Hrothgar. They reach the Danish coast and are directed by the watchman to Hrothgar's abode (lines 194-319). There the Danish king tells of his friendship with Beowulf's father Ecgtheow and Beowulf states the purpose of his coming. Then the visitors are invited to a feast (lines 320–497). At the banquet one of Hrothgar's followers Unferth speaks tauntingly to Beowulf and our hero retorts by relating his successful contest with a certain Breca in swimming (lines 498 – 606). Thereupon Hrothgar's queen, Wealhtheow, fills Beowulf's cup and the hero utters his determination to conquer the monster or die. Soon it grows dark and the king and his retinue depart, leaving Beowulf and his men to guard the hall (lines 607 – 665).

Then the first adventure begins. Before Beowulf and his companions get ready to go to sleep, the former puts off his armour and declares not to use his sword in the coming combat. Soon enough Grendel bursts into the hall and very quickly eats up one of the warriors and comes directly to Beowulf. The hero then engages in a terrific battle with the monster as the hall rings with the sound of their combat. Eventually Beowulf tears an arm and a shoulder off the monster who runs away, mortally wounded (lines 665 – 833). The victor displays Grendel's torn arm and the Danes show their admiration by telling stories of the heroes of the past. Then Hrothgar comes and rewards Beowulf with rich gifts (lines 834 – 1062). At the feast that follows, Hrothgar's minstrel sings of old tales (lines 1063 – 1159), and the queen appears and thanks Beowulf and presents him with a valuable necklace which is later worn by Hygelac and becomes the property of the Franks after the latter's death (lines 1160 – 1232). Hrothgar and Beowulf now retire while a number of warriors stay on in the hall for the night. Then Grendel's mother comes and carries off Aeschere, the king's chief councillor (lines 1233 – 1306). Beowulf is sent for and Hrothgar tells him of the tragic event and describes the abode of the monsters and Beowulf promises to avenge Aeschere (lines 1306 – 1396).

The second adventure opens with Beowulf and his companions setting out for a pool and upon arrival he plunges into the water and reaches a cave underneath. There he engages in a long struggle with Grendel's mother and finally succeeds in killing her with a magic sword of the ancient giants hanging in the cave. He cuts off her head as well as that of her son Grendel lying dead nearby. With these as his booty he returns to the shore of the pool where his companions are still waiting, already in despair about his life (lines 1397 – 1631). The victors march back to Heorot and are welcomed by Hrothgar who eulogizes the hero but then enters into a lengthy moralizing discourse on the evils of pride (lines 1632 – 1784). The next day Beowulf bids farewell to Hrothgar who rewards him with further gifts and the visiting warriors embark to return to their native land (lines 1785 – 1921). Then, after a laudatory account of the virtues of Hygd, King Hygelac's young wife, we are told of the meeting between Hygelac and Beowulf at which the latter first speaks digressively of the relations between Hrothgar and his daughter Freawaru and son-in-law Ingeld, and then gifts are exchanged between uncle Hygelac and nephew Beowulf (lines 1922-2199). After a lapse of time Hygelac dies and his son succeeds to the throne but is soon killed in battle by the Swedes. Then Beowulf is chosen king and he rules gloriously over the Geats for fifty years (lines 2200 - 2210).

The third and last adventure of our hero takes place in his own country. A dragon has kept guard over a hidden treasure hoarded for many years but suddenly finds part of the hoard stolen by a runaway slave, and in revenge he starts to ravage the land with the fatal blasts of his fiery breath. Beowulf, now an aged king, resolves to fight with the dragon himself (lines 2210 - 2349). But before the description of the battle, lengthy digressions are introduced. First there are reminiscences by our hero, as he recalls how at a battle in the land of the Frisians Hygelac lost his life while Beowulf himself escaped by swimming, how upon his return therefrom he refused the throne offered him by Hygelac's widow-queen Hygd, how young Heardred succeeded his father Hygelac but was soon slain by the Swedish king Onela and finally how Beowulf some time later avenged the death of Heardred by participating in a feud that led to Onela's death (lines 2349 - 2396). Then, the main thread of the story is resumed with an account of Beowulf taking with him twelve companions and approaching the shore dwelling of the dragon, but a second digression is inserted as the old king recollects the more remote past of his family history: how one brother of Hygelac's, Haethcyn, then the king of the Geats, accidentally killed another brother Herebeald, how their father Hrethel died of grief in consequence, how subsequently in a war with the Swedes Haethcyn and the Swedish king Ongentheow, Onela's father, were both killed, how Hygelac the third brother died among the Frisians, and how there Beowulf killed Daeghrefn a warrior of the Hugas (lines 2397 - 2509). Then when the main narrative is picked up again, Beowulf orders his men to wait outside while he goes down to the mound of the hoard where the dragon lives. There he is attacked by the dragon and his sword fails him when he uses it to pierce the monster's scales. Beowulf now falls under the threat of the fiery breath of the dragon and is in great danger, but one of the companions Wiglaf, son of Weoxstan, rushes down to help while the other companions flee into a wood. In the meantime Beowulf strikes at the dragon on the head, but his sword breaks and the dragon seizes him by the neck. In the nick of time Wiglaf succeeds in wounding the dragon and Beowulf kills the monster with his knife (lines 2510 - 2709). But the old king is himself mortally wounded, and as Wiglaf brings the treasure out of the hoard, the king gives his last orders about his own funeral and presents the faithful companion with his armour and necklace and then dies (lines 2709 - 2842). The cowardly warriors now return and Wiglaf rebukes them and sends a messenger to the people to announce the king's death. The messenger in his speech foretells the disasters that are to follow Beowulf's death, recalling the former wars with the Franks, the Frisians and the Swedes and prophesying future strife with these enemies now that the hero is no longer alive to protect his people. Then the people arrive at the scene of the fight and carry away the treasure hoard. Wiglaf repeats Beowulf's dying instructions, and the dragon is thrown into the sea as a funeral pyre is built on which Beowulf's body is burned. Over his remains a huge mound is piled up and the dragon's treasures are placed therein. Twelve warriors ride round the barrow lamenting the death of Beowulf and praising his virtues as a great and good king: "of all kings he was the gentlest and most gracious of men, the kindest to his people and the most desirous of renown" (lines 2842 - 3183).

Except for occasional digressions when the hero recalls past events or when some gleeman sings a tale, "Beowulf" as a poem centres on the narration of the exploits of the heroic figure Beowulf, including his adventures with Grendel and his mother in Denmark and with the dragon in the land of the Geats. In other words, it is a long verse narrative on the theme of "arms and the man" and as such belongs to the tradition of a national epic in European literature that can be traced back to Homer's "Iliad" and Vergil's "Aeneid".

Another characteristic of the epic tradition to be found in "Beowulf" is the part-historical, part-legendary origin of the story. It's part-historical as quite a number of the characters either appearing or mentioned in the poem are real persons lifted from the pages of history, including King Hrothgar of the Danes (based on "Historia Danica" of Saxo Grammaticus) and King Hygelac of the Geats (based on "Historica Francorum" of Gregory of Tours and "Gesta Regum Francorum" as well as "Liber Monstrorum"), both of whom play rather important roles in the development of the tale. Besides, several digressional episodes in the epic, those about Finn and Hnaef (in the gleeman's lay) and about Ingeld and Freawaru as well as the one about the wars between the Swedes and the Geats, all have their historical basis. And these historical figures and events place the poem in the historical period of the disintegration of tribal society, when there were tribal wars as well as inter- and intra-family feuds among the rulers. But the hero Beowulf is essentially a legendary figure. His name cannot be found in any historical document, and all that scholarly research can do has been to try to identify him with Beowa, a deity in Northern Mythology known to have killed sea monsters and dragons, or to compare him with Sigmund or his son Sigurd (alias Siegfried) in the "Edda" or "Volsunga Saga" or "Nibelungenlied", though his relations with Hygelac and the Geat people and with Hrothgar and the Danes all appear to be rather realistic reflections of the social conditions of the tribal age during which the poem must have been first conceived and sung. Also, Beowulf's fights with Grendel and Grendel's mother and the dragon, all with a distinctly mythical or fabular character, have their parallels in other European legends, and they also illustrate the common desire of the tribal people in ancient times to conquer the mysterious forces of nature that wrought havoc upon human society.

There can be little doubt that the development of "Beowulf" as an epic, from its oral tradition to its present written form, took up several centuries. The fact that the locale of the story is set in Denmark and southern Sweden shows all too clearly that the tale was brought over by the Angles, Saxons or more likely Jutes from their Continental homes upon their immigration to England. Therefore, while the epic contains chiefly reflections of tribal society in a heathen world, there are also many feudal elements in it and some Christian colouring. For instance, while the chief theme of the poem is the primitive people's struggle against hostile forces of the natural world under a wise and mighty leader and there are gleeman's tales of tribal wars and inter- and intra-family feuds and of intimate kinsmen's relationship between the kings and their warriors, yet on the other hand the kings described not only were already hereditary but were possessed of absolute authority to have big halls built and hold feasts there and dispense gifts to his guests and followers. The warriors or thanes were loyal subjects of the king and were ever ready to risk their lives for their sovereign, and they resembled somewhat the feudal knights as they sallied forth on their adventures to kill monsters and dragons in order to relieve the distressed. Also there is in the poem obvious censure here and there of the bloody feuds among the kinsmen in the ruling circles. Even the story of the runaway slave's robbery of the hoard of gold and of the dragon's revenge for the loss is a motif that has its many parallels in other old legendary tales in European poetry (e.g., the "Nibelungenlied") and belongs to the feudal age rather than to the earlier days of tribalism.

Likewise, the curious mixing in the poem of pagan elements with Christian colouring was the natural result of the epic descending from its original oral form and passing through the hands of a number of different scribes from generation to generation. The most striking example is the frequent reference in the epic to "wyrd" (i.e., fate) as the decisive factor in human affairs, but at other times and in different places there is also the mention of "God" or "Lord" as the omniscient and omnipotent being that rules over the whole universe. Sometimes the poet-singer even interrupts the narrative with uncalled-for interpolations to point to God's intervention in helping the virtuous and punishing the wicked or to lament the misfortunes of the heathens who were unable to see the invisible power of God everywhere. Direct but rather curious references to Biblical personages are also occasionally to be found, such as identifying the monster Grendel with "the children of Cain". Also, in Hrothgar's lengthy passages of moralizings following Beowulf's conquest of Grendel's mother and in the not infrequent comments here and there on the brevity and transitoriness of human existence, the influence of Christian religion is quite unmistakable, with its emphasis on moral behaviour and on the importance of "future life" above earthly bliss.

But, on the whole, the pagan mood is more dominant and tribal life rather than feudal ways seems to be the determining factor for the main structure of the story. However, though the tale deals with happenings on the European Continent, the extant written version of the poem grew up on the English soil and consequently must have absorbed much from the social life and manners of the Anglo-Saxons following their settlement in England, so it is not improper to consider the work as an early national epic of the English people.

Anglo-Saxon or Old English, in which "Beowulf" was written, represents the earliest stage in the history of the English language and is very different from modern English. It appears almost like another language altogether and cannot be understood today by English-speaking peoples unless one consults notes and glossary in detail or reads its translation in modern English. It was closely related to Old Low German and therefore it is highly-inflected like other Germanic languages. "Beowulf" was written in alliterative verse, employing the device of alliteration instead of the use of rhymes or blank verse that was common to the English poems beginning from the Middle English period. In the practice of alliteration, words beginning with the same consonants alliterate with each other within each line, or a word beginning with a vowel alliterates with another word beginning with the same or another vowel. Each line of verse may contain an indefinite number of words or syllables but generally has four stresses, with a pause between the second and the third stresses, thus breaking the line into two parts. Alliteration invariably falls upon the stressed syllables, but not all four of the stresses in a line need to alliterate, usually two or three of them alliterate, with at least one from each half-line. The first three lines of the original poem are given here as specimen, with their translation into modern English provided below:

Hwaet! we Gar-Dena   in gear-dagum
péod-cyninga   prym gefranon,
hupa aeð lingas   ellen frémedon.
(Lo! we Spear-Danes in days long past
Of warrior kings'   glory have heard,
How the princes   wrought deeds of prowess.)

One peculiar characteristic of style in "Beowulf" is the frequent use of compound-words to serve as indirect metaphors that are sometimes very picturesque. These are known as "kennings", such as: "swan-road", "whale-path" or "seal-bath" used to refer to the sea; "wave-traveller" to indicate a ship; "shield-bearer", "battle-hero" or "spear-fighter" as substitute for the word "soldier"; "sword-clashings" or "edge-clash" to describe battlings or fights; "ring-mail", "limb-sark" or "breast-net" as equivalent to armour.

"Beowulf" towers above all other literary works written in Anglo-Saxon, chiefly because it is a powerful poem about a people's hero written in true epic style, and not so much because the other extant writings of the period are mediocre or fragmentary. Beowulf is not simply a man of great military prowess but he is forever eager to help others in distress and in his last adventure with the dragon he shows himself a worthy leader ready to sacrifice his own life for the welfare of his people. Setting aside the supernatural elements pervading the poem as an inevitable limitation of the tribal-feudal age, "Beowulf" deserves to be ranked among the great heroic poems of northern Europe though it has not been as well known as the "Nibelungenlied". In artistic form the epic tells the tale in a leisurely way, full of elaborations in legendary details, and the verse rises at places to heights of poetic grandeur, particularly in the descriptions of the hero's nobility of character and in the narrations of his courageous battlings with malevolent foes.

3. Minor Anglo-Saxon Poetry: Caedmon and Cynewulf.

Besides "Beowulf", other secular poems of the Anglo-Saxon

period are of little significance, most of them short and some fragmentary. Of narrative verse, there are two older poems based on Germanic legends brought from the Continent: (1) two fragments of "Waldhere" or "Waldere", dealing with events connected with the story of Waldhere in the "Nibelungenlied", and (2) "The Fight at Finnsburg", a fragment about legendary material mentioned in "Beowulf". There are two other verse narratives of later date having to do with battles fought on the English soil: "Brunanburg" about the battle fought in the year 937, and "The Battle of Maldon", fought in 993. Of lyrical poetry, two of the earliest extant Anglo-Saxon songs, "Widsith" (probably of the 7th century) and "Deor's Lament" (probably of the 8th century), are good literary specimens illustrating the life and social position of the "scops" or "gleemen" of late-tribal, early-feudal times, the first a minstrel's own narration of his successful career with the different princes and kings he visited while the second the selfaccount of a once popular poet-singer falling into disgrace when a rival of greater skill wins the favour of his master. Of later lyrics mention may be made of "The Seafarer" and "The Wanderer", both dealing with adventures on the sea, and of "The Wife's Complaint" and "The Lover's Message" (or "The Husband's Message"), perhaps the two earliest love poems in the English language, the former lamenting the loss of the poet's love while the latter declaring the writer's faith and steadfastness in love. It is interesting to note here in passing that there's been a modern English rendering of "The Seafarer" by a 20th-century American poet, Ezra Pound, which reads like an original piece rather than a translation but which contains the alliterative verse form of Anglo-Saxon poetry. A very different kind of verse is "Ruin", a melancholy poem on the past glories of a ruined site. Then there were a series of 95 Anglo-Saxon "Riddles", similar to the riddles in Latin and varying in length from one line to over a hundred. Of these only a few are worthy of note, including those on natural phenomena,e.g.,the riddles on "Wind" and "Storm", which are picturesque and lyrical and contain rich and brilliant sketches of life of the Anglo-Saxon people.

The bulk of Anglo-Saxon verse now extant is religious or Christian poetry. The most colourful figure among the Christian poets of the period is unquestionably Caedmon whose story was told only in the "Ecclesiastical History" of the venerable Bede, a monk at Jarrow, and to whom a number of poems have since been attributed. According to Bede, Caedmon was a cowherd of a monastery at Whitby, in Northumberland, who with no gift for singing generally left the feasts at the monastery when the harp was passed around and every one was asked to sing in turn. But one night when he returned to the stable to take care of the cattle and fell asleep, in a dream someone stood by him, called him by name and asked him to sing, and when he said he could not sing, he was told to sing of the creation of the world, and he immediately began to sing in praise of God the Creator. After he woke up, he remembered the words of the song sung in his sleep, and later others told him stories from the Bible which he could not read, and they asked him to put the stories into poetry and the following morning he composed the passages in excellent verse. This was of course only a story, one that involved a miracle, but because Bede was considered a reliable historian and Whitby was very near Jarrow, the impossible story was accepted by many Christian believers of the day as true, though today it is even open to question whether such a poet as Caedmon ever existed. But even according to Bede, only the first "Hymn" was supposed to have been definitely composed and sung by Caedmon in the form of a Latin paraphrase of nine lines, and this when rendered into modern English verse is nothing more than a common hymn and falls far short of great poetry. The other poems attributed to Caedmon have generally been called by scholars "Caedmonian poems" and were very likely written by some anonymous authors.

Practically all these Caedmonian poems were no more than paraphrases of passages from the Christian Bible, and only the second of the two versions of a poem entitled "Genesis" (known as "Genesis B") deserves attention. The two versions make up the complete poem of altogether 2935 lines that deals with the story in the first book of the Old Testament. "Genesis B" comprises of lines 235–851 that were interpolated into the first version of "Genesis A" and describes Satan's overthrow and then the temptation and fall of Adam and Eve. Here the figures of Satan and of Adam and Eve are vivid portraits of human beings and their thoughts and feelings are carefully examined into. The two episodes of Satan's call for rebellion and revenge and of the gradual yielding of Adam and Eve to temptation are particularly interesting, especially the former. First, Satan utters his thoughts of revolt against the bondage of slavery as follows:

"Why, then should   Not a shred of need
    I toil? quoth he.   there is
Now for me to have a   With these hands of
    master!   mine I may
work as many wonders! Mickle wielding force have I
For the setting up   Of a goodlier stool than he
Higher in the Heaven! Why should I at all, for His favour
         be His slave,
Bow to Him in such a I a god may be, like Him
    bondage?
With me stand strong- Who will nevermore, the
   hearted comrades,   struggle fail me;
Heroes hardy-hearted!"
         (lines 278 – 285 from "Genesis B", a Caedmonian
         poem, translated into modern English by Stopford A.
         Brooke)
And then, after Eve has taken the fruit from the tree of knowledge, she is described as having been awakened to a new world of beauty:

    "Sheener to her seemed   All the sky and earth;
    All this world was lovelier; And the work of God,
    Mickle was and mighty then, Though 'twas not by man's
              device
    That she saw (the sight) … "
   (lines 603 – 606, from "Genesis B", translation by Stopford
   A. Brooke)
Though the poem as a whole is enveloped in an intense atmosphere of religious exhortation, the two episodes partly quoted above at least

reflect on the one hand the keen desire for knowledge among the common people in England at the time and on the other hand the thoughts of rebellion among the erstwhile free tillers of the earth under tribalism who were being shackled under the bondage of serfdom in Anglo-Saxon Britain. What is more important, Satan's call for revolt against slavery not only has its significance in representing the English serf's desire for freedom from oppression, but in a curious way also anticipates the similar speeches made by Satan in the first two books of Milton's "Paradise Lost".

Another poem preserved in the same manuscript as "Beowulf" and attributed to Caedmon is "Judith", which some scholars however consider as more closely related to the school of the later poet Cynewulf. It is a fragment, with only its 10th, 11th and 12th books and a part of the 9th preserved. Here the climax of the story is given, as the colourful Jewish heroine Judith goes to the enemy camp, hews off the head of the invading Assyrian general Holofernes and thus saves her people from their foreign aggressors. The story is taken from the Apocrypha, and though there isn't much great poetry here, at least the heroism of a clever, courageous and patriotic girl risking her life for her people is vividly described.

Cynewulf is even more of a mythical figure than Caedmon, the only reliable fact about him being the appearance of his signature in runes in four Anglo-Saxon poems: "Juliana", "Christ", "Fates of the Apostles" and "Elene". The most probable date of his life has been assigned to the last quarter of the 8th century or to the 9th, and he is believed by many to be a Northumbrian. Besides the four above-mentioned poems, a number of others have also been attributed to him or to his school of poetry.

"Christ" is Cynewulf's best known poem. It has three parts: the first dealing with the coming of Christ on earth (i.e., his nativity), the second with his ascension (including his crucifixion and ascension to heaven), while the third with his second coming to judge the world (i.e., the Day of Judgment). The contents of the poem are strictly religious and follow rather closely the traditional Christian lore, yet there are some realistic passages on nature, especially on the sea and the winds, that must have been based on the poet's personal experience, besides bits of fine dramatic dialogue, such as that between Joseph and Mary at the time of Christ's nativity, derived apparently from the author's observations of life in Anglo-Saxon society.

The two poems "Juliana" and "Elena", as well as two others attributed to Cynewalf, "Guthlac" and "Andreas", are all based on the legends about the lives of the Christian saints, Guthlac being a native English saint while the other three of Byzantine background. Here English scenes and manners are depicted though in three of the poems the poet was supposedly dealing with stories of Continental environment in earlier history. Other Anglo-Saxon poems attributed to Cynewulf or to his school of poetry all deal with religious subjects or contain strong religious colouring, though some of them (like the poems "Phoenix" and "Physiologus" or "Bestiary") are interesting as poems on nature, particularly on the animal world, "Phoenix" relating the curious life of the mythical bird in its happy dream-land while "Physiologus" telling stories about the panther, the partridge and especially the whale, together with delightful descriptions of the sea.

4. Anglo-Saxon Prose: Bede; Alfred; "The Anglo-Saxon Chronicle"; Aelfric.

The earliest prose written in Anglo-Saxon England was in Latin, known sometimes as Anglo-Latin writings. Among these early writers of Latin prose should be mentioned Aldhelm or Ealdhelm of the second half of the 7th century (650? – 709), of Wessex, and Alcuin of the second half of the 8th century (735? – 804), of Northumbria, and the giant among them, the Venerable Bede (or Baeda) of Jarrow in Northumbria in the last part of the 7th and the early half of the 8th century (673? – 735).

Brought up in a monastery and remaining in that environment all his life, Bede was made a deacon at the age of 19 and a priest at 30 and he performed the regular duties of a Benedictine monk up to his last illness. He wrote numerous works on all kinds of subjects, including grammatical and critical handbooks, scientific treatises, commentaries on various books of the Bible, homilies, saints' lives and verse, all in Latin, many of which had wide circulation in medieval Europe, but his fame rests chiefly upon a historical work of his later years, "Historia Ecclesiastica Gentis Anglorum" (rendered into English as "The Ecclesiastical History of the English People"), published in Latin in 631 and later translated into Anglo-Saxon by King Alfred in the year 891.

With his "Ecclesiastical History" Bede earned his place as "Father of English History". The book covers practically the whole stretch of early English history, from the Roman invasion of Britain under Julius Caesar in the first century B.C., to A.D.731, four years before the author's death, and it has remained to this day the most important source book on this historical period. Here Bede showed his great love of truth in his serious attitude and meticulous care toward authenticity in the execution of the work. With the help of his assistants he examined all available records, secured verbal and written accounts from reliable living authorities, recorded local traditions and stories, and interpreted significant events, all in order to compile as complete and continuous a history of the English church and people as lay within his power. Of course, the book relates history largely from the religious point of view and is full of strange stories and miracles, but such a shortcoming is inevitable considering the author's profession and environment and the popular belief in miracles in his day. Occasional passages in this prose work contain elements of poetry, such as the famous episode about Caedmon the poet, but generally speaking a direct and simple style was employed.

In the early stage of the Anglo-Saxon period, in the 7th and 8th centuries, English culture and learning flourished in the north, particularly in Northumberland, with Bede and Alcuin in the lead, but in the later centuries, the 9th and the 10th, the centre of learning shifted to the south, to the Kingdom of Wessex, where King Alfred was the most prominent figure.

Alfred had the opportunity of visiting with his father and brothers the papal court at Rome and the French court at Paris when still a child. This experience in the then cultural centres of Europe must have left a strong impression upon him and later led to his eagerness to introduce culture to his own people. Then the invasion of the Danes brought about the destruction of the established centres of culture in Northumbria and East Anglia, and even the Kingdom of Wessex was threatened. In the year 871 Alfred became the king of Wessex upon the death of his brother Aethelred who fell in battle with the Danes. In 878 when much of Wessex was lost to the invaders along with the rest of England, Alfred withdrew to Athelney among the deep-watered marshes of Somersetshire and remained there for several months to gather an army. Then he came forth and attacked the Danish army and forced them to surrender, and a peace agreement was reached according to which Alfred and his men were to have the south of England (including the kingdoms of Wessex and Kent and the western part of Mercia) while the northern and eastern parts of the country remained under the rule of the Danes and were known as the Danelaw. The peace lasted for almost fifteen years up till 893, interrupted only once in 885 – 886, and these intervening years were made ample use of by Alfred, first to reform the army and build a navy and establish a sound system of government and law, and then to educate the people and introduce culture to the nation. He collected around him a number of scholars, including some invited from abroad, who first taught him Latin and then did translation work together with him, from Latin. Those were fruitful years for the development of early English culture under the direction of Alfred. In 893 war again broke out and it lasted till 897 when Alfred gained a conclusive victory, and he died four years later, in 901.

Alfred's contributions to English literature are threefold. First, there were his numerous translations from Latin of which four major works were particularly useful in his day: (1) Pope Gregory the Great's "Cura Pastoralis" ("Pastoral Care", 889), (2) Bede's "Ecclesiastical History" (890 – 891), (3) "The History of the World" ("Historia adverses Paganos") (891 – 893) by Paulus Orosius, a Spanish priest of the 5th century, and (4) "The Consolations of Philosophy" ("De Consolatione Philosophiae") (897-898) by Boethius, who was known as "the last of the Romans" (i.e., the last great writer of ancient Rome). To the translation of Gregory's "Pastoral Care", the least important of the four from the literary point of view, was affixed a "Preface" by Alfred, which has been considered by some as "the first important piece of prose in English". Here Alfred not only lamented the decay of learning in Britain and expressed his determination to reform the schools of Wessex, but he also defended the use of the vernacular and pointed out the necessity of making translations from Latin. The translation of Orosius' "History of the World" was to provide the English people at the time with the knowledge that they much needed of the history and geography of the world at large. The translation of Bede rendered a great service by making a great book on English history available to the common people who could not then read the original in Latin. With the translation of Boethius' "The Consolations of Philosophy" Alfred introduced a very influential book by a prominent writer which interprets the Platonic and Stoic doctrines of ancient Greece and mixed them with Christian philosophy. These and other translations served to introduce to the English people the cultures of other historical times and other lands.

A second contribution of Alfred's lies in his rather free way in translating from the Latin works, and this helped him to write in a natural style in English. Except in a few cases, he took liberties with the original writings by making alterations and additions and omissions wherever he thought fit, leaving out superfluous details and even turning out-dated information into current views of his own day. In these translations and his prefaces to them Alfred also contributed to the development of English prose by regularizing wherever possible the old elliptical abrupt style in the Latin language and thus preventing obscurity and lack of continuity in the expression of ideas.

Alfred's third contribution to English literature was the role he played in the launching of the "Anglo-Saxon Chronicle". Alfred first conceived the idea of a national history for England in about 891 and started organizing for the transcription of the old records or "Annals" of the kingdoms of Wessex and Kent (preserved at Winchester and Canterbury) and for further compilation, and as the project steadily grew and was carried on long after Alfred's time, it became known as the "Anglo-Saxon Chronicle", a very important historical document and specimen of Anglo-Saxon prose.

"Anglo-Saxon Chronicle", also known as the "Old English Chronicle", began with the year "A.D.1" and was carried on at several different centres after Alfred's death till as late as A.D. 1154, almost a century after the so-called Norman Conquest in 1066. The first part of the work deals with the first six centuries of the Christian era and is very sketchy, with only 9 entries for 9 of the years between A.D. 100 and 400 and many very brief entries comprising only one or two lines. The stretch from the 7th century to the 9th contains fuller records, especially in the period just before and during the time of King Alfred. And because the year-by-year entries continued to be compiled after Alfred's reign in several different places, the seven extant manuscripts of the "Chronicle" come from the different localities of Winchester, Abingdon, Worcester, Canterbury and Peterborough, thus showing the work to be the result of collective efforts of many persons of different times and places and accounting for the diversity of the "Chronicle" both in the choice and treatment of historical material and in the literary form and style employed. And because all the different versions of the "Chronicle" were apparently written by the monks or the clergy and were preserved in the monasteries, there is a distinctly religious colouring in most of the entries. But the most significant thing about the "Anglo-Saxon Chronicle" is that it represents, on the whole, the thoughts and feelings of the common people of England, particularly in the entries between the middle of the 10th century to the middle of the 12th. First of all, many poems and ballads are included that definitely belong to the tradition of folk literature. Also a common item in the entries is the mention of bad weather, such as severe winters and strong winds, and of famines and diseases of cattle, all of which led to the rise of the price of crops and consequently to great miseries for the people. Another common phenomenon in the "Chronicle" is the frequent mention of unusual sights or happenings in the natural world that must have aroused interest among the common people of the time, such as the eclipse of the sun or the moon, the appearances of the comet or shooting stars, earthquakes and certain superstitious phantasmagoria like "fiery dragons", "fiery lights in heaven" or"bloody rain". Of special interest are the numerous comments on the different kings in England, obviously from the point of view of the common people. The comments on four of the kings of the Anglo-Saxon period after Alfred are all in the form of short-lined verse. While all four of them were eulogized, King Edgar (or Eadgar) (959 - 975) was criticized:

> One misdeed he did,
> Too much however,
> That foreign tastes
> He loved too much;
> And heathen modes
> Into this land
> He brought too fast;
> Outlandish men
> Hither enticed;
> And to this earth
> Attracted crowds
> Of vicious men.

(Taken from an entry under the year A.D. 959, in the "Anglo-Saxon Chronicle")

More significant are comments made on four Norman kings, of whom William I was criticized as follows:

"So very stern was he and also hot, that no man durst do anything against his will. ... He was fallen into covetousness, and greediness he loved withal. He made many deer-parks; and he established laws therewith; so that whosoever slew a hart, or a hind, should be deprived of his eyesight."

(Taken from an entry under the year A.D. 1087, in the

"Anglo-Saxon Chronicle")

William II was more severely criticized:

"He was very harsh and severe over his land and his men and with all his neighbours; and very formidable; and through the counsels of evil men, that to him were always agreeable, and through his own avarice, he was ever tiring this nation with an army, and with unjust contributions. For in his days all right fell to the ground, and every wrong rose up before God and before the world. ... And for this he was loathed by nearly all his people, and odious to God as his end testified."

(Taken from an entry under the year A.D. 1100, in the "Anglo-Saxon Chronicle")

Above all, the "Anglo-Saxon Chronicle" contains a number of passages describing the terrible political oppression and economic exploitation that the common people suffered at the hands of their foreign invaders or their native rulers. In the entries for the 9th and 10th centuries there is frequent reference to the plunder by Danish invaders in the form of "tributes", and when King Edward the Confessor abolished the Danegeld in the year 1050, the "Chronicle" records:

"That tax distressed all the English nation during so long a time, as it has been written; that was ever before other taxes which were variously paid, and wherewith the people were manifestly distressed."

Then, in the entry for the year 1087, after a description of "a very heavy and pestilent season in this land" that year when many people died of diarrhœa and of hunger from famine, King William I and his followers are censured for their exploitation of the people:

"The king and the head men loved much, and overmuch, covetousness in gold and in silver; and recked not how sinfully it was got, provided it came to them. ... They erected unjust tolls, and many other unjust things they did, that are difficult to reckon."

Under the year 1104, during the rule of King Henry I, a similar passage is recorded:

> "It is not easy to describe the misery of this land, which it was suffering through various and manifold wrongs and impositions, that never failed nor ceased; and wheresoever the king (i.e., Henry I) went, there was full licence given to his company to harrow and oppress his wretched people; and in the midst thereof happened of ten times burnings and manslaughter. All this was done to the displeasure of God and to the vexation of this unhappy people."

But the most powerful attack on the terrible oppression and exploitation of the common people appears in an entry under the year 1137, during the reign of King Stephen:

> "Every rich man built castles, which they held against him (i.e., King Stephen): and they filled the land full of castles. They cruelly oppressed the wretched men of the land with castle-works; and when the castles were made, they filled them with devils and evil men. Then they took those whom they supposed to have any goods, both by night and by day, labouring men and women, and threw them into prison for their gold and silver, and inflicted on them unutterable tortures; for never were any martyrs so tortured as they were. Some they hanged up by the feet, and smoked them with foul smoke; and some by the thumbs, or by the head, and hung coats of mail on their feet. They tied knotted strings about their heads, and twisted them till the pain went to the brains. They put them into dungeons, wherein were adders, and snakes, and toads; and so destroyed them. Some they placed in a crucet-house; that is, in a chest that was short and narrow, and not deep; wherein they put sharp stones, and so thrust the man therein, that they broke all the limbs. In many of the castles were things loathsome and grim, called 'Sachenteges', of which two or three men had enough to bear one. It was thus made; that is, fastened to a beam; and they placed a sharp iron (collar) about the man's throat and neck, so

that he could in no direction either sit, or lie, or sleep, but bear all that iron. Many thousands they wore out with hunger. I neither can, nor may I tell all the wounds and all the pains which they inflicted on wretched men in this land. This lasted the nineteen winters while Stephen was king; and it grew continually worse and worse."

There can be no question that these passages are truthful descriptions of the state of things in Anglo-Saxon England and must have been written if not by some one among the common people, at least by some monk or clerk close to the labouring people and capable of knowing their woes and their hatred for the ruling class at the time.

And from the passages quoted above, we can see that the "Anglo-Saxon Chronicle" not only provided records of the people's life and their miseries, but was written in simple, straightforward language.

Brief mention should be made of Aelfric, called Grammaticus (c.965-c.1020) who wrote in the last decade of the 10th century and the early years of the 11th and has sometimes been considered the greatest prose writer of the century and a half between the death of King Alfred and the Norman Conquest in 1066. He was at first a monk at Winchester, then in 987 he was sent to the Abbey of Cerne in Dorsetshire as novice-master to instruct the monks there, and in the years 987 – 989 he began translating Latin books into English. He returned to Winchester and in 990 – 994 he issued two collections of homilies, each forty in number, under the title of "Homiliae Catholicae". These homilies were to serve as sermons for Sundays and feast-days and they gave a large survey of biblical and ecclesiastical history. Here the mystical elements of the Christian religion are emphasized, with much symbolism, and all the homilies contain alliterative passages while a small number are actually in alliterative verse, written as prose. In 1005 Aelfric was appointed the abbot of a monastery at Egnesham, near Oxford, where he lived a quiet life till his death in about 1020.

Aelfric also wrote a Latin grammar ("Grammar"), a Latin-English vocabulary ("Vocabulary" or "Glossary") and a Latin colloquy or dialogue ("Colloquium"), all of which were intended to instruct the novices in the monastery at Winchester. The most interesting book of the three, "Colloquium", is in the form of a conversation between the teacher, a novice, and a number of other persons representing the various occupations of the day, including a ploughman, a neatherd, a shepherd, a hunter and a merchant, and the living conditions of the people of that age are reflected in the conversation.

In 996 or 997 appeared a third series of homilies, entitled "The Lives, or Passions of the Saints" ("Passiones Sanctorum"), which included 33 lives, 6 general homilies and a narrative without a title on the legend of Abgarus, making up a total of forty pieces. Aelfric also made a translation or paraphrase in Anglo-Saxon of the first seven books of the Bible (the Heptateuch) and wrote a treatise "Concerning the Old and New Testament" ("De Veteriet de Novo Testamento") which served as a popular introduction to the contents of the Bible in Old English.

While Aelfric's writings are chiefly religious in content and therefore of little interest to us today, they were nevertheless very influential at the time of their publication, and in the historical development of English culture and literature his writings not only were instrumental to the extension of education and learning, for the clergy as well as for the laity, but they were also important specimens of a clear, flexible and popular Anglo-Saxon prose though many of his homilies resembled alliterative verse.

Chapter II

ENGLISH LITERATURE OF THE LATE MIDDLE AGES

SECTION I   ENGLISH LITERATURE FROM THE MID-11TH CENTURY TO THE MID-14TH.

1. The Background: Political and Social.

The Norman Conquest of 1066 accelerated the development of feudalism in England. Many Normans who came with William I were given large tracts of land that had been confiscated from the Anglo-Saxon nobility and other recalcitrant landlords, and they became feudal barons or vassals to the king and in turn allotted their land possessions to their own vassals. Though William I made all his vassals and his vassals' vassals swear allegiance to himself directly, the big barons still had much political power and could raise troops to fight among themselves or even to resist the king. The Magna Carta of 1215, which many bourgeois historians have claimed as the beginning of democracy for England, was actually no more than a document of concessions made by King John chiefly to the feudal barons and the potentates of the Church, and only to a very small extent to the rising plebeians. The ecclesiastics, from the monks and the clergy to the bishops and archbishops, together possessed over one third of the land in the country and owned numerous serfs, and had their tithes and ecclesiastical courts and the backing of the Pope in Rome. They had much political as well as religious power and ranked together with the big feudal barons as important participants in the affairs of the state.

The chief social conflict in England in the three centuries after the Norman Conquest was inevitably that between the serfs or peasants and their feudal lords though some historians are inclined to think that the struggles and wars among the feudal barons and between the barons and the king were the major contradiction of the time. But all scholars have to admit that the terrible oppression and exploitation of the serfs by the feudal rulers led to many peasants fleeing from the countryside to the growing cities and towns, and that other serfs armed themselves and destroyed the manors of their feudal lords or at least got organized and refused to pay heavy rents on the land or to carry out their enforced tasks of labour. The Hundred Years' War with France which began in 1337 led to the drafting of soldiers from among the peasantry and to the levying of extra taxes upon the poor labouring masses, thus intensifying the sufferings of the serfs. The Black Death of 1349-50 swept across the country and brought about the scarcity of labour in the countryside, but in answer to the peasants' subsequent demands for higher wages, laws known as the "Statutes of Labourers" were passed in parliament in 1351, 1357 and 1361, imposing heavy punishments upon all peasants that refused to work at the old rates for their feudal lords. All these prepared the way for the large-scale peasant risings in the second half of the 14th century.

After the Norman Conquest England became no longer an isolated nation and trade relations with the European Continent grew steadily. There were rapid developments in commerce and handicraft industry in the newly established towns and cities, and the burgesses, made up of petty tradespeople and artisans many of whom were former peasants, gradually became a political force to be reckoned with, especially the citizens of the nation's capital and biggest city, London. Beginning from 1165 these burgesses were represented in parliament and as time went on they played an increasingly important role in the nation-wide political struggle.

The three centuries following the Norman Conquest saw the large-scale introduction into England of French culture, including French customs and manners, medieval French literature and the literature of Italy and other European countries, as well as the extensive use of the Norman-French language, particularly in the cities and the big manors where the Norman nobility lived. For almost two hundred years after 1066, two languages, native English and Norman-French, existed side by side in England, together with Latin. While the native English tongue, descended from Anglo-Saxon or Old English, was the common speech of the overwhelming majority of the people, especially of the peasants in the countryside and among the lower ranks of the trades-people and artisans in the towns, French for quite a long time prevailed at the king's court, in the big manors, in the lawcourts and in the bigger schools where Latin was also taught, and the clergy and many scholars made use of Latin in the churches and monasteries and ecclesiastical courts. By the mid-14th century the English language finally gained absolute supremacy in the whole country, particularly with the passage in parliament in 1362 of the Statute of Pleading, according to which it was required that court proceedings be conducted henceforth in English. But by then the English language had already been totally different from Old English, for in the three centuries after 1066 the language had undergone gradual but radical and extensive changes, as not only were borrowed in the course of time thousands of words from French and through French from Latin and also Greek, but many old inflectional forms of native English words had been dropped and formal grammar of the past had become considerably simplified. The English language in this transitional stage from Old English to modern English, through some four centuries (from 12th to 15th) of development and change, has generally been known as Middle English.

2. Folk Literature and Religious Literature from the Mid-11th to the Mid-14th Century.

As a result of the simultaneous use of three different languages, English, Norman-French and Latin, in the centuries after 1066, there were in England a number of literary works written in Norman-French and in Latin besides those in English. In Anglo-Latin literature of the period, possibly the most important writer was Geoffrey of Monmouth, a Welshman and an archdeacon whose "Historia Regum Britanniae" ("The History of the Kings of Britain"), written in 1136, not only provided the earliest full account of the legends of King Arthur and his Round Table knights and Merlin but for the first time brought to the attention of English readers and writers the stories of Lear, Cymbeline, Gorboduc, Ferrex and Porrex, Locrine and Sabrina, that were later to inspire Shakespeare and other Elizabethan dramatists and Milton in their dramas and poems. Next should be mentioned the colourful figure of Roger Bacon (1214 – 1292), who has been known to many as "the father of experimental science" and as a most versatile scholar, linguist, philosopher and scientist. He wrote chiefly in Latin ("Opus Maius", "Opus Minus" and "Opus Tertium"). Of these works "Opus Maius", as a sort of encyclopaedia of facts concerning the sciences of the time, is more important.

There were numerous writings in England in the field of Anglo-Norman or Anglo-French literature in this period, extending from romances to fabliaux, from political poems and satires to religious works and legends of lives of saints, from lyrics and "debates" to drama, but outstanding writers were few. In the field of romances, Marie de France, a French writer of some importance and a collector of the Arthurian legend, did part of her work in England, while Benoît de Sainte-More wrote the "Roman de Troie" which dealt with the tale of the Trojan war and provided material for the story of Troilus and Cressida later used by Chaucer and Henryson and Shakespeare. Then a number of political poems and satires written in French by Anglo-Norman writers also deserve mention. There were some satires on the church, particularly those touching on the notorious vices of some of the monks (e.g., "L'Ordre de Bel Aise"). Poems were also written to attack the heavy taxes levied at the time (e.g., "Against Taxes"), and sometimes the church as well as the king were satirized for tax-levying (e.g., "A Song of the Church", 1256).

In Middle English literature from the mid-11th to the mid-14th century, folk literature took precedence over religious writings and romances. First should be mentioned a few social satires in verse. In the "Song of the Husbandman", written toward the close of the 13th century and in strophes of alternately eight and four lines, with both alliteration and rhyme, we hear the voice of the English peasant of the time complaining of his miseries under the oppression of the bailiff and the burden of taxation to support foreign wars. All kinds of officials are said to be squeezing profit out of the poor labourer so that he is robbed and picked "ful clene" and is hunted "as hounds do the hare on the hill", with the result that "who once wore robes, now wear rags", and "Thus breed many beggars bold". Another lyric on the same theme is "A Song against the Retinues of the Great People", in which is told in bitter and sarcastic words the insolence of the grooms and the stableboys, the lackeys and servants, and all the so-called retinues of the great people, in their dealings with the peasantry.

There were also a number of satires specially directed at the clergy. Of these the incomplete poem of 476 long lines, "On the Evil Times of Edward II", is particularly significant. Here the poet first describes war and hunger and poverty and the rise in the price of corn and puts the blame chiefly upon the clergy. Some bishops and archbishops are described as fools who lead a sorry life and dare not reprove their clergy for fear of being betrayed themselves. Archdeacons take bribery of each other and let the parsons and priests have wives. When a clerical post is vacant it is sold to the highest bidder, and the one who buys the post gathers money and rides out of town with hawks and hounds into a strange country where he dwells comfortably, leaving his church to a thief and a whore. Though a bishop knows of the evil behaviour of his reckless subordinates, a little money will stop his mouth. Abbots and priors counterfeit knights, and pride is master in every house of an order of monks. The poor are kept out of the monasteries, while the monks dress comfortably and give themselves up to ease and gluttony and become fat and red-cheeked. The friars preach more for a bushel of wheat than to save a soul, and in shrift they discriminate between the rich and the poor. They even fight for the corpse of a rich man. Then the poet turns his satire from the clericals onto other members of the ruling class. False physicians help men to die, they pretend that a man is sicker than he is, deceive the wife to get money for the medicines, and themselves eat the good dishes she prepares. Instead of going to the Holy Land, the earls, the barons and the knights dispute with one another at home. Squires are no longer gentlemen, but profane and false. Justices "will do wrong for meed", while sheriffs, mayors and bailiffs all deserve the lash of scorn. The king is deceived by them, for his officials are all cheats. The attorneys, chapmen and assisors are also deceitful. The poor are pillaged, browbeaten and oppressed. The extensive exposé here of the social evils of the day is unusual, anticipating more effective social criticism in the works of Langland and Chaucer of the late 14th century.

Of other satirical poems on the vices within the church, mention may be made of: (1) "When Holy Church Is Under Foot" where the prevalence of simony, i.e., the buying and selling of ecclesiastical preferments, is attacked and the writer points out that the church is now despised by all because even the Pope is guilty of bribery; (2) "Satire on the Monks and People of Kildare", a poem of the 13th century, in which various saints, ecclesiastics and tradespeople are described sarcastically; and (3) "Sir Penny" where the theme that money can do everything suggests faintly the figure of Lady Meed in William Langland's "Piers the Plowman". Yet another well-known satire directed chiefly at the monks is "The Land of Cokaygne". This poem was written in the medieval French tradition of a fabliau, i.e., a short story in verse relating some comic incidents of ordinary life, and here the poet wrote sarcastically about the land of Cokaygne as a monk's paradise, which is actually a land of gluttony and idleness and lechery.

Aside from the social satires, the pride of place in folk literature of the period should be given to the popular lyric, with nature or love as the theme. The best known lyric on nature is surely the "Cuckoo Song" (c.1300) in which the simple outburst of joy is felt by the common folk in the countryside upon the return of spring and is uttered in a spontaneous note and a free rhythm:

"Summer is y-comen in!
Loud sing cuckoo!
Groweth seed and bloweth mead,
And springeth the wood new.
Sing cuckoo! cuckoo!

Ewe bleateth after lamb,

> Loweth after calfe cow;
> Bullock starteth, back verteth;
> Merry sing cuckoo!
> Cuckoo! cuckoo!
> Nor cease thou ever now.
> Sing cuckoo now!
> Sing cuckoo!"

Another charming and fresh lyric on nature (and also love) is "Spring-time" which begins thus:

> "Lent is come with love to town,
> With blossoms and with birdës roun.
> That all this blissë bringeth;
> Daisies in these dales,
> Sweet notes of the nightingales,
> Each fowl song singeth."

Of love lyrics of the time possibly the most famous is one entitled "Alysoun" of which the first stanza is especially delightful:

> "Between March and April,
> When spray beginneth to spring,
> The little fowl hath her will
> On the land to sing,
> I live in love-longing
> For seemliest of allë thing.
> She may me bliss bring.
> I am in her bandoun. (power)
> A hendy hap I have yhent, (a strange thing has hap-
>   pened to me)
> I wot from Heaven it is me sent,
> From all women my love is lent, (turned)
> And light on alysoun." (alighted on Alysoun)

There is grace in the simplicity of language in these lyrics, and the verse rhythm and rhymes employed with the short lines are particularly suitable to the sentiments expressed.   The influence of the troubadour tradition of love poetry in Provence is here quite unmistakable, for in spite of their apparent simplicity these lyrics belong rather to the category of art-songs and as such they anticipated the outbursts of lyrical songs on love and nature that were to flourish in England in the 16th century.

Although in the three centuries after 1066 there were numerous religious works in Middle English both in verse and prose, although a few of them, like Robert Mannyng's "Handlyng Synne" (1303), the anonymous "Cursor Mundi" ("The Course of the World", c.1320) and Richard Rolle of Hampole's "The Prick of Conscience" (1340), were widely read and had much influence in their day, yet all of them deal with religious subjects that had no true significance at the time nor are of interest to us today. There were also some didactic poems, of which "The Pearl" is the best known. It is an allegorical poem of 101 stanzas of 12 lines each, with both alliteration and rhyme, and relates the vision of one who has lost a pearl. The poem contains rich imagery in the descriptions of the poet's visions, and the personal feelings of the author toward his lost pearl of a daughter are poignantly given and point to his reluctance to give up all the joys and sorrows of earthly existence, but the tale is marred by lengthy explanations of the Christian doctrines of salvation and by reiterated exhortations to man's strivings for otherworldly bliss.

3. Early Alliterative and Metrical Romances in the 12th, 13th and Early 14th Centuries.

Romances, alliterative and metrical, constitute the bulk of the literary works in England in the three centuries after 1066. The word "romance" here refers to some verse narrative that sings of knightly adventures or other heroic deeds, and usually emphasizes the chivalric love of the Middle Ages in Europe. Most of the English romances deal with three major themes: "The Matter of Britain", about the Arthurian legend; "The Matter of France", about stories concerning Charlemagne and his knights; and "The Matter of Rome", about tales of antiquity, from the Trojan war to the feats of Alexander the Great. There were of course also some native English tales dating back to the time of the invasions of the Vikings on the English coast, as well as other miscellaneous stories and legends. English romances of this period are, generally speaking, inferior and less colourful than similar verse narratives at about the same time in Germany and France, such as the "Chanson de Roland".

Most of the English romances of the time were metrical, metre and rhyme having been adopted from French poetry to take the place of alliteration in Anglo-Saxon poetry, but in early 14th century there was a curious revival of alliterative verse in a number of romances written in the West Midland dialect of Middle English.

The legend of King Arthur and his Round Table knights was the most popular theme employed. The origins of the Arthurian legend are very complicated and even confusing because there was an Arthur as a historical figure ("dux bellorum", i.e., "the leader of the wars") of the Celts in a series of 12 battles to repulse the invading Anglo-Saxons; then there was another Arthur as a mythological figure appearing chiefly in Welsh literature as a king of fairy-land, who undertakes hazardous quests, slays monsters, visits the realms of the dead and has a number of knightly henchmen; and finally there was an Arthur as a legendary hero reported by Geoffrey of Monmouth in his Latin "Historia Regum Britanniae" (1137). In this last book the main framework of the now commonly known Arthurian legend is sketched, beginning from the prophecies of Merlin and the birth of Arthur, through his marriage with Guanhumara (Guenevere) and his various conquests and knightly adventures, to the treachery of his nephew Mordred and his battle with the latter, and finally to Mordred's defeat and Guenevere turning nun and Arthur himself mortally wounded and carried to Avalon. Geoffrey of Monmouth's book was translated by more than one writer into French and then Layamon, a humble priest on the banks of the Severn, told the Arthurian story for the first time in English in his alliterative poem with occasional rhymes, "Brut" (1205). In the meantime, in the late 12th and early 13th centuries the Arthurian legend became very popular on the European Continent, particularly in France and Germany, as it was retold with elaborations by German poets Wolfram von Eschenbach and Gottfried von Strassburg and French poets Marie de France and Chrestien (or Chrétien) de Troyes. So that by about 1300 most of the legendary material woven round the story of King Arthur and his Round Table knights, from Merlin and the birth of Arthur, to Guenevere and the treachery of Mordred and the passing of Arthur, and including the heroic deeds of the best known knights like Lancelot and Tristram, Gawain and Percival as well as the story of the Holy Grail, had all been treated of whether in chronicle or in romance, in verse or in prose, in English or in Welsh or in Latin, French or German. The Arthurian romances written in English were mostly metrical, usually dealing with one particular knight or another, with Tristram and his love for Iseult, with Ywain and Gawain, with Lancelot and the maid of Astolet, with Percival and the Holy Grail, and with Merlin and Arthur himself, but before the whole story was gathered together in a continuous thread in Sir Thomas Malory's "Le Morte d'Arthur" in the 15th century, perhaps the most outstanding single romance on the Arthurian legend was the anonymous "Sir Gawain and the Green Knight", written in 1360–1370, in alliterative verse.

"Sir Gawain and the Green Knight" contains four "fits" or sections. In the first fit, King Arthur is holding at Camelot his Christmas feast of 15 days with all his knights of the Round Table. The New Year comes and Arthur and his queen Guenevere and all the knights are seated at the table, but the king refuses to eat before he witnesses a "wondrous adventure" of some sort. Suddenly there rushes in a knight, the tallest on earth, clothed all in green and riding a green horse. He carries neither spear nor shield but a holly bough in one hand and in the other an axe with its edge as keen as a sharp razor. Arthur welcomes him and the knight utters the challenge to any one brave enough to strike him a blow with the axe and to receive a return blow "within a twelve-month and a day". Fear keeps all the men there silent for a while. Then just as Arthur feels bound to seize the axe himself, Sir Gawain comes forward and asks permission to answer the challenge. The king gives his nephew the axe and the green knight lays bare his neck and Gawain lets fall the axe and severs the head from the body. The head falls to the ground but the knight falters not. He picks up the head and steps into the saddle and the head speaks to Gawain, asking him to seek for the Green Knight at the Green Chapel to receive the return blow the next New Year's morn. The Green Knight departs and Arthur and his knights go on with their feasting.

The second fit begins with a lengthy description of the passing of the four seasons, from spring through summer and autumn and back to winter again, and Arthur makes a feast to send Gawain off on his journey. Then follows a detailed account of all the accoutrements made ready for the knight before he takes leave. Gawain rides on his horse Gringolet through the realm of England to North Wales and gets no answers to his inquiries for the Green Knight of the Green Chapel. He climbs over many cliffs and crosses many fords and streams and meets with all sorts of adventures with serpents, wolves and wild men, with bulls and bears, and the sharp winter brings special hardships. Soon it is Christmas-eve and he prays to the Virgin Mary, and soon he finds himself in a deep forest of many old oaks and sees in the wood on a hill the comeliest castle. He calls aloud and the drawbridge is let down and he is received into the castle and welcomed by the lord there-in. He is shown to a chamber well decorated with curtains and tapes-tries, and he is given fine clothes and fine food and is entertained by the lord of the castle and his wife, fairer even than Guenevere, with an old lady beside her. Gawain tells his host of his errand to meet the Green Knight, and when he is told that the Green Chapel is not more than two miles away, he agrees to stay on at the castle till the New Year's Day. Then the lord of the castle makes a bargain with Gawain that for each day of his stay at the castle, the guest and the host are to ex-change with each other at night what they gain during the day.

The third fit tells of the three days of Gawain's sojourn at the castle. The first day the host goes to hunt with a hundred hunters and many hounds and they kill many deer. Sir Gawain lies abed and is visited by the fair lady of the castle, but he resists temptation and only lets her kiss him once. At night the host gives Gawain the venison of the deer he has slain and Gawain gives him a kiss. The second day the host hunts again and he and his fellow-hunters pursue a wild boar. The lady of the castle visits Gawain again and teases him for being a renowned knight and yet not knowing how to make love to a lady, but Gawain defends himself and the lady leaves after kissing him once again. The host returns with the boar killed and at night he gives Gawain the shields of the boar and Gawain again kisses the host. The third day the host goes hunting again and this time he hunts a fox. The lady of the castle comes again to entice Gawain, kissing him and desiring some gift from him. Gawain again resists and declines her gift of a gold ring. She offers him a second gift, this time her girdle, which he refuses at first, but when she says the girdle has the magic power of protecting the wearer from being wounded or slain, Gawain wavers upon the thought of his imminent encounter with the Green Knight and is finally persuaded to accept it as a secret gift. Then the lady kisses him thrice and departs. Gawain conceals the girdle on his person and goes to mass and shrives himself of his misdeeds. The host that night gives Gawain the skin of the dead fox while Gawain gives him only the three kisses. Then the guest thanks the host and his lady for his happy sojourn at the castle and goes to bed, ready to proceed to the Green Chapel the following day.

The fourth fit begins with a description of the stormy snow weather on the New Year's Day as Gawain gets ready to go to the Green Chapel. Taking with him the girdle, he thanks the host at parting and a servant of the castle leads the way. They reach a high hill and the guide persuades Gawain not to go forward, for the Green Knight is terrible and has killed many. But Gawain refuses to be a coward and so the guide now leaves him, after telling him the way to the Green Chapel. Gawain goes alone and finally finds an old cave in the crag. He hears a loud noise and the Green Knight appears to demand the return blow according to the covenant. Gawain bares his neck but shrinks a little as the axe comes down and the Green Knight reproves him. Upon the second blow Gawain does not flinch and the axe pierces the flesh and blood flows. Then the Green Knight reveals himself to be no other than the lord of the castle, and he reproves Gawain for having concealed the girdle given him by the lady. Gawain is confounded, takes off the girdle and throws it at the other, and curses his own cowardice and covetousness. The Green Knight forgives him and gives him back the girdle, and reveals his own name to be Bercilak de Hautdesert and the older lady in his castle to be Morgan le Fay, Arthur's enemy. He asks Gawain to go back to his castle, but Gawain refuses and he returns to Arthur's court and tells the king and all the other knights of his adventures, feeling ashamed as he relates of the girdle and the cut in his neck. The king and the whole court comfort him and each of the knights agrees to wear a bright green belt for Gawain's sake.

Though there are no descriptions of battles or jousts, the two main motifs in the story, the tests of faith, courage and purity and the human weakness for self-preservation, that point to the nobility as well as the humanness of the hero, provide the poem with unmistakable traits of chivalric romances, plus some strong Christian colouring.

Besides, the romance gives the reader an engrossing tale well told, vested in beautiful poetry and containing many artistic merits, such as the careful interweaving of one episode with another, the elements of suspense and surprise as the story unfolds itself, the psychological analysis of the chief character Sir Gawain as he encounters one strange event after another, the elaborate descriptions of the seasons as well as the places and things witnessed by the hero in the course of his adventures and finally the simple, straightforward language employed. Therefore, the popularity of the poem over and above most other romances of the period is well-grounded. As for the introduction here of supernatural elements and superstition, that was no more than a natural and inevitable limitation of the age in which the poem was written. However, the heroic adventures of Sir Gawain and of King Arthur as related in the poem were sought after and carried out rather for adventures' sake than any truly worthy cause, and in this sense the romance in its true significance falls short of a poem like "Beowulf" where the heroic deeds were performed to help the hero's kinsfolk out of their distress or to protect them from disaster.

Of the native English romances, brief mention need be made of "Guy of Warwick" (c.1300) and "Havelok the Dane" (c.1250). Both poems follow the conventional pattern of a hero performing knightly deeds of prowess and rising eventually to princely position and power. In "Guy of Warwick" the titular hero was not born a prince but was the son of an earl's steward who succeeded in winning the love of the earl's daughter and becoming a national hero simply because he helped King Aethelstan in defeating Colbrand the Dane and thus rescued England from her foreign invaders. In "Havelok the Dane", the hero was born of a prince's family, but his wicked guardian usurped the kingdom and handed over the boy Havelok to a fisherman named Grimm to be drowned. The child was however saved by the fisherman and his wife and they fled together to England. Havelok was brought up as a fisherboy to sell his basket of fish. Then he served as a kitchen boy in an earl's household where he distinguished himself by his great strength and athletic proficiency. He was married to an English princess who was likewise robbed of her inheritance by a treacherous tutor. In the end he regained his own kingdom and conquered England also. The story ends on a conventional note, but the descriptions of Havelok as a fisher-boy and then as a kitchen help and the story of his happy relations with the poor children and the cook indicate the author's sympathy for the labouring people which was quite exceptional for most poets of that time.

SECTION II ENGLISH LITERATURE OF THE SECOND HALF OF THE 14TH CENTURY.

1. The Background: Political and Social.

Mounting feudal oppression in the second half of the 14th century led to the peasants' revolts. The long drawn-out Hundred Years' War begun in 1377 called for extra taxes. The Black Death that came first in 1349 – 50 and then again and again in the 1360's reduced the whole population by almost a third and with the dearth of available farmhands their original wages were naturally doubled and trebled. Then the ruling class thrice passed the so-called Statutes of Labourers in parliament, stipulating that all able-bodied men and women under sixty be required to work for any one at the rate of wages fixed in 1347 or before, and that those who refused to do so be arrested or declared outlaws. On top of this, heavy land-rents and enforced services were practised as before, and consequently many peasants fled from the land to the towns while some went to the forests and organized themselves as bandits or outlaws. After Richard II became king, three times he asked the parliament to pass new poll taxes (in 1377, 1379 and 1381). All these events led inevitably to the great peasants' rising in 1381. It began at Kent and Essex and spread to other parts of the country and the peasants finally came and took London. Richard II played a dirty trick on the peasants by promising to redress their wrongs but he quickly killed their leaders Wat Tyler, Jack Straw and John Ball and disarmed the insurrectionaries and forced them to go home. But though the rising was thus quelled by the treacherous king, the popular discontent had its effect in the abolition of enforced services on the land as well as other laws of medieval serfdom, so that there was actually no more serfdom in England by the end of the 14th century.

The misdeeds and atrocities committed by the royal family and the big feudal nobles against the peasants were matched by those perpetrated by the clergy at the time. The church owned almost a third of all the land in the country and the clergy as feudal landlords were often very terrible and extortionary. They also made use of their ecclesiastical courts to oppress the common people and to squeeze as much money as possible out of them. Some of the big abbots and monks led extravagant and even lecherous lives, while the several orders of friars as well as the pardoners who sold pardons and the summoners who summoned sinners to the church courts likewise did all they could to cheat the people and extract money out of them. The church tithes and other ecclesiastical dues also were heavy burdens to the poor, and except for the few poor parish priests who were close to the people, most of the clericals cared little for preaching or the welfare of their parishioners, but often tried their best to obtain better church jobs by bribing and flattering the religious magnates. So the clergy were not infrequently the chief butt of satire in the literary works of the time. Of course there were some few good priests who tried to reform the church, as for instance John Wycliffe and his followers known as the Lollards.

Commerce and manufacture grew apace and brought wealth to the towns and cities and consequently also power to the more wealthy burghers, especially to the citizens of London who began to play an important role in national politics and to be feared by the king. These burghers had their representatives in parliament and they could refuse to pass laws and grant subsidies to the king before their grievances were redressed. In the cities the distinction between the rich and the poor gradually became more marked, and the wealthy citizens together with the rich noblemen and the royal household led lives of extravagance while many poor people starved and lived in extreme destitution. The corruption of government officials was also rife at the period.

Chivalry was rapidly losing its glamour though romances were still written in the latter part of the 14th century to celebrate the knightly deeds of the past. The early flowering of the Renaissance, begun in Italy in the 13th century, soon spread to France and by the end of the 14th century the writings of Petrarch and Boccaccio already started to exert their influence upon many English writers. Superstition prevalent through the Middle Ages was beginning to lose ground in the minds of the people with the gradual dawning of science in Europe, and medieval magic and astrology came to be somewhat discredited, at least among the educated few.

The second half of the 14th century marked the deterioration and decline of feudalism in England and the big economic and political changes had their impact upon literature. In this half-century, English literature flourished after three centuries of comparative lull, and the chief writers of the period were John Wycliffe, John Gower, William

Langland and above all, Geoffrey Chaucer.

2. John Wycliffe; John Gower; William Langland.

John Wycliffe (or Wyclif) (1324? – 1384) was born in Yorkshire. He went to Oxford in about 1345 and became Master of Balliol College in 1360. He spent years of study on theology, and in 1368 became rector at Ludgerhall, near Oxford, and then in 1372 he got his degree of Doctor of Theology at Oxford. He gradually was drawn into the struggle between King Edward III and the Pope in Rome. At first he only opposed the right of the Pope to make levies on England and to appoint foreigners to English benefices, then he proceeded to attack the whole system of church government, opposing the right of the church to own land and other property, rejecting papal authority by advocating the absolute authority of the Bible, and attacking episcopal privileges and the religious orders of friars as well as the abuse of indulgences, pardons and sanctuary. Later the king and the nobility began to turn against him. Especially after the peasants' rising of 1381, some of Wycliffe's doctrines were condemned at an assembly of bishops and ecclesiastics and then he was suspended from all scholastic duties and had to leave Oxford. In the last years of his life he continued to inspire his "poor preachers", the founders of the Lollard sect, and to develop in a series of Latin and English works the doctrines which later came to be associated with Puritanism. In 1384, struck down by paralysis, he died.

From the literary point of view Wycliffe's chief contribution lies in his responsibility for the earliest translation of the entire Bible from Latin into English. Though he probably only distributed the work of the translation among his followers at Oxford, he was certainly the guiding spirit of the task. His original writings were mostly in Latin. In "De Veritate Sacrae Scripturae" ("Of the Truth of the Holy Scriptures") he insisted on the absolute authority of the Bible. In "De Dominio Divino" ("Of Divine Dominion") and "De Civili Dominio" ("Of Civilian Dominion") he stated the view that the clergy has no right to hold property and that the condition for the exercise of all authority is righteousness without which none should have power.

Wycliffe's English writings include his sermons and a number of treatises. The former, used in his time as models for his followers the "poor priests", were different from the ornate and rhetorical popular pulpit orations of the time by being sober, practical and full of common sense. One of his English treatises, "Of Servants and Lords", possibly inspired by the peasants' rising of 1381, is most significant. Here, while he insists on the mutual obligation between the servants and their lords, he describes the numerous ways in which the poor people were wronged in those days by the rich rulers.

Wycliffe had much influence while lecturing at Oxford because at that time many intellectual youths flocked to the university to learn new ways of thinking, and Wycliffe's lectures and pamphlets directed against papal authority as well as corruptions inside the church paved the way for a more thorough-going reformation in the church in the later centuries. More important still was Wycliffe's influence upon the "poor priests" who later developed into Lollardy and had their effect upon revolutionary thinking at the time and even directly upon the peasants' rising of 1381. Though the Lollards held more drastic views than Wycliffe's, yet his ideas on church property developed into those of the Lollards' against the entire feudal system in the distribution of wealth. His denunciation of the evils inside the church became for the Lollards a hatred of the whole church, while his appeal to the Bible as the ultimate test of everything grew into his followers' disregard for the whole hierarchy of the church and their faith in the Bible as the only authority. So when the peasants' rising came in 1381, his "poor priests" were charged with having incited to it, and John Ball, one of the leaders of the rising and a clergyman, is said to have confessed at his trial that he had adopted his views from Wycliffe.

John Gower (1330? – 1408) belonged to a knightly family in Kent, and probably possessed two other manors in Norfolk and Suffolk. He spent most of his time in London and was connected with the court and known personally to Richard II and John of Gaunt, though he apparently never held any office in the government. He devoted much of his time to literature and wrote with equal ease in three languages, English, French and Latin. Late in life he appears to have married. He went blind in 1400. The peasants' rising of 1381 must have affected the poet whose main estate was in Kent.

Gower is known for his three chief works written in three different languages: "Speculum Meditantis" or "Mirour de l'Omme" in French (1376 – 79), "Vox Clamantis" in Latin (c.1382) and "Confessio Amantis" in English (1390 – 93). "Mirour de l'Omme" ("The Mirror of Mankind"), first discovered in 1896, is a long poem of about 29,000 lines, a religious allegory in three parts on the sins of man. In the more significant second part, there are vivid pictures of the corruption of the church from top to bottom and of the great miseries of the labourers, though the author's chief thought was to show how all men, including the clergy and the secular rulers and dignitaries as well as plebeians and labourers, were corrupted by sin.

"Vox Clamantis" ("The Voice of the Clamants") refers quite definitely to the peasants' rising of 1381. In the first part of the poem, through the literary device of a vision and a dream, Gower describes a swarming mass of people laying waste Troynovant ("New Troy", referring obviously to London) and speaks of a jay named Wat (alluding to Wat Tyler, the leader of the peasants' rising of 1381) whose death breaks the strength of the group. Here the poet even compares the popular rising to beasts ravaging the countryside and creating terror and disorder, and his mention of one boar coming from Kent and another from the north bringing destruction wherever they go was a very definite allusion to Tyler from Kent and another peasant leader Jack Straw from Essex. And a third leader of the peasants' rising, John Ball, was attacked here in the reference to an "excommunicate priest" who preaches the text, "When Adam delved and Eve span, who was then the gentleman?" The author's strong antipathy toward the peasants' rising is unmistakable.

In the second part of "Vox Clamantis", though Gower continues to speak strongly against the discontent of the peasants and accuses them of being irrational like beasts, he tries to explain the peasants' rising as God's punishment on men for their sins and proceeds to censure the vices of the clergy, from the papal court at Rome to the monks and the friars and the rectors in the parishes, and to attack the degenerate knights and bribe-taking lawyers and sheriffs and bailiffs and even the royal court of Richard II as the centre of all vices. Then in the last part of the poem Gower turns from his descriptions of the corruptions of the English society of his time to a thoroughly unrealistic picture of feudal England of the earlier Middle Ages and falls into religious moralizings on the prospect of the Day of Last Judgment and the need to repent for one's sins.

Taken as a whole "Vox Clamantis" voices Gower's vicious attacks on the peasants' rising of 1381 from his standpoint of a feudal landlord but in the meantime, quite in spite of himself, he gives here a partly realistic picture of the social evils of the day, especially in the second part of the poem.

Gower's only major poem in English, "Confessio Amantis" ("A Lover's Confession"), is a long work extending to 33,000 lines of octosyllabic couplets and contains a collection of 120 verse-tales to illustrate the seven deadly sins, with a prologue and an epilogue to link them up. The main structure of the poem is conventional, with Gower himself as the "lover" who makes his confession to Genius, the priest of Venus, and the stories as exemplary tales of love are chiefly adapted from classical and medieval sources. The author shows himself to be a good story-teller and excels particularly in picturesque descriptions. As a medieval English poet in the tradition of courtly love and moral allegory, Gower once enjoyed a reputation matching that of his friend and contemporary Geoffrey Chaucer, but his popularity waned after the 16th century.

William Langland (or Langley) was born in about 1332 in Shropshire. His father was possibly a farmer and he himself was probably educated for the church at Malvern. Later he went to London and lived for many years at Cornhill. He seemed to be in minor orders, or may have been conversant with the writing of legal documents and may have eked out his subsistence by the small sums gained that way. There are many allusions in "Piers the Plowman" to the author's extreme poverty. He died in about 1400. "Piers the Plowman" is extant in upwards of 50 mansucripts, and this testifies to its great popularity both at the time of its publication and afterwards. These manuscripts have generally been grouped into chiefly three different versions, the A, B and C texts, dated 1362, 1377 and 1393 - 8, respectively, and containing 2567, 7242 and 7357 lines of verse, with the B text preferred by most scholars to the other two.

The poem has often been divided, for the sake of convenience, into two parts: 1. the vision of Piers the Plowman, and 2. the vision of Do-wel, Do-bet and Do-best. The poem opens with the usual medieval literary convention of vision and allegory. On a May morning the poet falls asleep upon the Malvern Hills and dreams. He sees a tower on a hill in the east and a dark dungeon of evil spirits in the west and between the two "a fair field full of folk", the rich and the poor, the clergy and the laymen. There are plowmen who work hard and play seldom, and there are merchants and craftsmen, bakers, brewers, butchers, tailors, tinkers, weavers of linen, cooks and kitchen lads, and beggars and jugglers and jesters and harmless minstrels. Different types of religious folk are then described at some length: the clergymen and wandering hermits who are loath to work and wish to have an easy life, pilgrims and palmers and friars and pardoners and corrupt priests all of whom lie and cheat and use religion for their own profit, and bishops and deacons, masters and doctors, who "lie in London, in Lent, ay, all the year." The lawyers are also satirized, while the king and his knights are depicted not unfavourably.

Then the vision is resumed and the dreamer sees a lovely lady, Holy Church, who tells him to seek for Truth in order to save his soul. The dreamer then sees Falsehood and Flattery and between the two a woman wonderfully clothed, Lady Meed (here "Meed" obviously means Bribery), and Falsehood is to marry her the next day. The wedding is arranged, supported by Flattery and Simony and Civil-law but objected to by Theology. Flattery bribes lawyers and others with gold, and they all go to London to bear witness at the marriage before the court at Westminster. The king, informed of their coming, threatens to catch Falsehood and his fellows and hang them. Falsehood is warned and the whole crew flee in all directions. Only Meed stays and is brought to the court. All the justices and clerks come to aid her and comfort her, and she rewards them with gold, silver and jewels in plenty. A confessor confesses her for a sackful of wheat, and she advises mayors and judges to take bribes. The king asks Conscience, one of his knights, to marry Meed, but Conscience refuses and exposes her faults. The king sends for Reason who advises the king to act with strict justice toward Meed. Meed is accused and the king asks Reason and Conscience to stay with him as his counsellors.

Here ends the first vision in the first part of the poem, and here the poet's social criticism is the keenest, directed particularly at the prevalent corruption and bribery in the English society at the time. Though enveloped in allegory, the poem contains unmistakable satire on practically all the different branches of the clerical profession(the summoners, friars, pardoners, confessors, monks, the pope and all the priests) and many of the lay authorities (justices and judges, lawyers and jurymen, sheriffs and clerks, mayors and merchants).

As the poem proceeds, the poet awakes but soon falls asleep again and has a second dream. Again he sees a field full of folk and Reason preaching among them. Many are affected by his sermon and the Seven Deadly Sins (Pride, Luxury or Lechery, Envy, Wrath, Avarice, Gluttony and Sloth) begin to repent and make their confessions one after another. After the confessions a thousand men come to seek for Truth but no one knows the way. Then Piers the Plowman appears, and says he has served Truth for fifty long years and will be their guide, but he must first plow his halfacre. Some of the pilgrims help Piers but many shirk from the work, and Piers threatens them with famine. The wasters challenge Piers to a fight. Piers calls for Hunger who reduces the wasters to subordination and they ask for work. Then Harvest comes and the Poor People feed Hunger and put him to sleep. The beggars and labourers demand fine bread and fresh meats and grumble about wages and curse the king and his council for the labour-law (obviously referring to the Statutes of Labourers). The author warns the workmen to earn while they can, for famine will return. Truth then sends Piers a message to go on with his work, and a pardon perpetual for him and his heirs. Part of this pardon is granted to kings and knights and bishops who fulfill their duties. Merchants are denied full pardon, lawyers obtain the least pardon, and tramps and beggars receive no pardon. The poor and the needy have full pardon. A priest disputes the validity of the pardon and a quarrel ensues. Piers tears up the pardon and declares he will no longer work so hard for worldly bliss but will engage himself in prayers and penitence. The dreamer awakes and the second vision ends.

This second vision shows Langland's great sympathy for the peasants and for the poor and the needy as well as his affirmation of labour and disapproval of idleness, but here the poet looks favourably at the "dutiful kings and knights and bishops" and distinguishes them from merchants and lawyers and tramps and beggars, and he also confuses the labourers' demand for more wages with the wasters' unwillingness to work and thus erroneously represents the peasants' righteous struggle against the Statutes of Labourers at the time.

The second part of the poem is much less important. In the visions of Do-wel, Do-bet and Do-best, many allegorical figures as well as Christ and Anti-Christ are introduced but little social significance is to be found in the allegory.

Taken as a whole, "Piers the Plowman", in spite of its conventional religious theme, its long drawn-out moralizings and its involved allegory and innumerable personifications, yet holds up a mirror to Langland's England, showing on the one hand the corruption prevalent among the ruling classes, both secular and clerical, and on the other hand the uprightness and worthiness of the labouring folk and the miseries of the poor and the needy. Pictures of terrible class struggle in late 14th-century England peep through many passages in the poem. The poor peasants are shown to be oppressed and exploited by the landlords, cheated by summoners, pardoners, friars, merchants and lawyers, and maltreated in every way by lay and clerical authorities, with the gates of the law-courts closed against them and the magistrates and bishops deaf to their complaints. And the poet's satirical comments on the different members of the ruling classes and his eulogies for Piers the plowman as the only guide in the pilgrims' search for Truth reveal clearly his own class leanings and reflect the popular sentiments in the age of the great peasants' rising of 1381. However, Langland's rather dubious allusion to the Statutes of Labourers points at least to the influence upon him of the ideology of the ruling classes of his day, and his generally favourable attitude toward the king and the knights reflects the illusory hopes of many common people of England placed upon the king as the possible redresser of social wrongs and shows also the surviving influence of the medieval tradition of chivalry and knighthood. And, in spite of the many satirical thrusts at the whole clerical profession, the Christian religion with its dogmas of Christ as the saviour and of the horrors of the seven deadly sins are still firmly believed in by the poet.

The influence of "Piers the Plowman" was wide-spread and long continued. A number of other satires were written shortly after it, partially or wholly in imitation. The participants in the peasants' rising of 1381 knew the early versions of the poem well and drew inspiration from it. John Ball, one of the leaders of the rising, referred, in his letter to the people of Essex, to Piers the Plowman and to Do-wel and Do-bet.

3. Geoffrey Chaucer.

Geoffrey Chaucer (c.1340 – 1400) was born of a wine-merchant's family, with rising fortunes and some standing at the court. In 1357 Chaucer served as a court page. Two years later he was in the English army fighting in France and was taken prisoner. After his release upon a ransom in 1360, he returned to England. Probably in 1366 he was married to Philippa, one of the demoiselles of the queen's chamber. From 1361 to 1367 he was a student at the Inner Temple where he received training for a career at the court. In 1367 he entered the service of King Edward III. For the next ten years diplomatic errands took him some nine times to the European Continent. His journey to Genoa and Florence in Italy from December 1372 to May 1373 was of particular significance, as it brought him into contact with the new tendencies of the Renaissance in Italian literature which were to exert considerable influence upon some of his subsequent work. One tradition has it that he met Petrarch in Padua while on this journey.

Besides these diplomatic missions Chaucer had other public employments. In 1374 he was made Controller of Customs and Subsidy of Wools, Skins and Hides, in the port of London. In 1382 he was appointed furthermore Controller of the Petty Customs on Wines and Other Merchandise. In 1385 he became one of the justices of the peace for Kent where he probably took up residence for some time, and in 1386 he was elected Member of Parliament for Kent. In October of that year he attended parliament and in December he no longer held his two posts at the Customs House. This last was probably due to the eclipse of the influence of his patron John of Gaunt at the court, which possibly also accounted for his later failure to be re-elected to parliament. The death of his wife in 1387 and the subsequent loss of her annuity led to a change for the worse in Chaucer's financial circumstances, and on May 1, 1388 the poet had to sell his own royal annuity to a certain John Selby for a sum of ready money. Then in 1389 he began to receive new preferments when Richard II came of age and John of Gaunt returned into favour. That year he was appointed to the important office of Clerk of the King's Works and had charge of buildings and repairs of the Tower, Westminster Palace and other royal residences as well as lodges, mews, parks, etc. Then in 1390, in addition to his regular duties as Clerk of the King's Works, he was also appointed to a mission to look after the walls, bridges, sewers and ditches along the Thames River from Greenwich to Woolwich. He must have been a very active man of affairs at that time, having had the management of a large number of workmen and a very considerable sum of money. There was record that in September, 1390, he was robbed more than once within four days and was on one occasion assaulted and beaten. He gave up the clerkship in 1391 when he was appointed deputy forester of the royal forest of North Petherton in Somersetshire and the appointment was renewed in 1398. After 1391 Chaucer also received a yearly pension from John of Gaunt, and a gift and then an annuity from Richard II and later Henry IV, though he is known to have several times during this period borrowed small sums of money from his friends and to have written poems about his poverty (e.g., "Complaint to His Purse"). In 1399 he took the lease of a house in the garden of Westminster Abbey, but he died shortly afterwards in 1400 and was the first to be buried in the Poet's Corner of Westminster Abbey. In his lifetime Chaucer served in a great variety of occupations. As courtier, office-holder, soldier, ambassador, legislator, burgher of London, he had broad and intimate acquaintance with persons high and low in all walks of life and knew well the whole social life of his time. And this varied career had its impact upon the wide range of his writings and particularly upon the variegated pictures of the English society of his time to be found in his masterpiece "The Canterbury Tales".

Chaucer's literary career may be divided roughly into three periods: the first period stretching from the 1360s to about 1372 during which time he fell chiefly under the influence of French poetry of the Middle Ages, the second period extending from 1372 to 1385 – 6 when the poet wrote under the spell of the great literary geniuses of early Renaissance Italy: Dante and Petrarch and Boccaccio, and the third and last period covering the last fifteen years of the poet's life (1386–1400) when he produced his works of full maturity free from any dominant foreign influence.

Chaucer's earliest work of any length is his "Romaunt of the Rose", a translation of the French "Roman de la Rose" by Gaillaume de Lorris and Jean de Meung, which was a love allegory enjoying widespread popularity in the 13th and 14th centuries not only in France but throughout Europe. Though we meet with a conventional allegory of courtly love in the tradition of medieval chivalric romance, yet unlike his fellow-poets Gower and Langland, Chaucer at least succeeded in detaching himself from the insipid atmosphere of medieval ecclesiastical literature and first introduced here into English verse the octosyllabic couplet.

Among Chaucer's original poems in his early period, the best known is "The Book of the Duchess", an elegy written upon the death in 1369 of Blanche, first wife of the poet's patron John of Gaunt. The theme here of the poet joining in a hunting company in a dream and of his meeting a knight who mourns the loss of his beloved virtuous lady is thoroughly conventional and is expressed in over-rich and ornamental language, but there are in the poem some passages of true pathos in the knight's lamentings over his lost love and occasional lines of delightful lyricism.

The second period of Chaucer's literary career includes chiefly the three longer poems written prior to "The Canterbury Tales": "The House of Fame" (in the 1370s), "Troylus and Criseyde" (1382 - 85) and "The Legend of Good Women" (1385 - 86). Of these "The Legend of Good Women" is again a love vision, beginning with an allegorical prologue of which there were two versions. In the longer version the poet in a May day dream is accused by Cupid the God of Love of having defamed women by translating the "Roman de la Rose" and writing "Troylus and Criseyde", and Chaucer in his penance promises to write year by year stories about faithful women. The nine "legends" about nine "good women" that follow were "tragedies" drawn from classical antiquity of women who suffered or died of devotion to their lovers and were borrowed from Boccaccio, Virgil and particularly Ovid. However, the poet seems to be voicing his disapproval of tyrannical kings when in the Prologue the fair queen Alceste led by Cupid the God of Love is made to declare at one place that "A righteous lord should have this (i.e., love) in mind, and not be like Lombard tyrants who practice wilful tyranny; for a king or lord by natural right ought not to be tyrannical or cruel like a farmer of taxes, doing all the harm he can." Here also was the heroic couplet used for the first time by Chaucer, or rather, used for the first time in the English language.

In the unfinished poem "The House of Fame", the poet dreams that he is carried away by an eagle and the Goddess of Fame in the House of Fame is described who in her sheer caprice gives her awards haphazardly to the crowds of people coming to ask for her favour. Then the House of Rumour is pictured where a multitude of people are busily relating from mouth to mouth what they have scarcely heard of and where a truth and a lie sometimes get mixed together and fly up as a piece of news to be blown out of the trumpets of Aeolus the god of winds. In this poem Chaucer delivers through rich fancy and humour his satire on fame in two different senses of the word: fame as glory or honour which according to the poet's suggestion depends more on sheer chance than on true merit and so is often granted to the undeserving, including the idle, the treacherous and the evil; and fame as rumour or gossip which the author considers as either based on something totally groundless or just a curious mixture of true and false tidings. And there is an abundance of typical Chaucerian humour in the dialogue between the poet and the golden eagle who carries him in flights hither and thither.

Though Troylus was mentioned in Homer's "Iliad" as one of the sons of the Trojan king Priam, the story of the two lovers Troylus and Criseyde (at first named Briseida) was not to be found in classical Greek or Roman tradition but it first appeared in the early Middle Ages in the Latin translations of the supposedly Trojan writers Dictys Cretensis and Dares Phrygius. Then the tale was told again in the "Roman de Troie" by the French poet Benoit de Sainte Maures in late 12th century, then in a Latin prose version "Historia Trojana" by a 13th-century Italian writer Guido delle Colonne, and finally in a long poem in ottava rima entitled "Il Filostrato" ("The Love-stricken") by the early Renaissance Italian writer Boccaccio. Chaucer's "Troylus and Criseyde" was partly adapted and partly translated from Boccaccio's poem, and in turn it inspired Henryson's "Testament of Cressid" in the 15th century, Shakespeare's "Troilus and Cressida" in early 17th century and John Dryden's adaptation of Shakespeare's drama with the same title during the Restoration.

The story in Chaucer's poem is supposed to take place during the Trojan War in ancient times. Troylus, son of the Trojan king Priam and a brave warrior as well as a scoffer at love, falls in love with

Criseyde, daughter of the soothsayer Calchas. Pandarus, Troylus' close friend and Criseyde's uncle, brings the two lovers together. Then Calchas who in the meantime has gone over to the Greek camp, persuades the Greeks to offer a Trojan prisoner Antenor in exchange for Criseyde. The lovers have to part, but Criseyde promises to return within ten days. Once she is in the Greek camp, a Greek warrior Diomede pays court to her, and when she finds it quite impossible to go back to Troy, she finally yields to her new lover. Troylus sees one day a coat wrested from Diomede in battle and on it he finds the brooch he once gave to Criseyde. Thereafter he seeks battle with Diomede and after killing many Greeks falls at last before Achilles.

While Chaucer tells this ancient Trojan tale somewhat in the spirit of the medieval chivalric romance, with Troylus and Criseyde appearing like a knight and a lady in courtly love, there are no allegorical personages nor supernatural elements in the poem but rather vivid portraits of a pair of passionate lovers in a late feudal and early bourgeois environment, thus anticipating the domestic dramas and novels of a much later date. Chaucer also improved upon Boccaccio by creating a more finely etched picture of Pandarus and by delving into the psychological world of the heroine Criseyde. The development of the plot is also more carefully worked out. However, like Boccaccio, Chaucer in combatting asceticism of an earlier age painted a number of rather risqué scenes of physical love that border on the coarse and the obscene. But there can be no question that Chaucer took a big step forward in the art of narration with his subtle characterization and engrossing plot.

"The Canterbury Tales", generally considered to be Chaucer's masterpiece, was written chiefly in the years 1387 – 1400. It begins with a general prologue that explains the occasion for the narration of the tales and gives a description of the pilgrims who narrate the tales, and then follow the twenty-four tales that make up the bulk of the book, plus the separate prologues and the "links" that accompany some of the tales. The work was obviously left unfinished upon the poet's death in 1400.

In the General Prologue which has usually been regarded as the most important part of the whole poem, the poet tells how, one day in April, he comes to the Tabard Inn in the southern suburb of London. By nightfall there arrive at the inn some nine and twenty pilgrims all ready to go to St. Thomas à Becket's tomb at Canterbury, and the poet joins the company and converses with all of them. At the proposal of Harry Bailey, the host of the inn, all the pilgrims agree that they make their journey to and from Canterbury more interesting by telling stories to one another on the way. Each of them is to tell two stories on the outward trip and two more on the way back. Whoever tells the best tale is to be given a free supper, at the cost of all the rest, upon their return to the Tabard Inn. The host offers to go with them as their guide and judge. According to this arrangement, there should be altogether a hundred and twenty stories in the collection, but actually only twenty-four tales are preserved, among which two are left incomplete, being interrupted as it were in the course of narration, while two others obviously remain unfinished.

"The Canterbury Tales" is not merely a collection of stories strung together by some loose thread, as was the general practice for some European writers of the late Middle Ages and early Renaissance to assemble a rather large group of tales into a single work of some magnitude, but Chaucer creates in the "General Prologue" to the "Tales" a whole gallery of vivid characters from all walks of life and then assigns to each of them some appropriate tale capable of shedding light on the respective narrator's distinctive personality, and then in the separate "prologues" to some of the tales and in the "links" linking up some of them the author makes further efforts to show the interplay between the characters as well as their respective traits and idiosyncrasies. Thus the total effect of the poem as a whole is a comprehensive picture of the social reality of the poet's day, especially since the pilgrims portrayed include men and women of all different professions, the high and the low, the lay and the clerical, the learned and the ignorant, the roguish and the upright, all excepting the very highest (i.e., the king and top nobility) and the lowest (i.e., the very poor labouring folk) in social rank at the time. As was natural in Chaucer's day a great variety of types represented among those going on the pilgrimage to Canterbury are connected with the church in some way or other: from the monastic orders we have a rich monk and a friar, a prioress with her chaplain, a nun and three priests while the secular clergy in the group includes a parşon, a pardoner and a summoner, to be joined later by a canon and his yeoman devoted to alchemy. From the upper rung on the social ladder we have a knight and a squire and a yeoman, a wealthy franklin, then a doctor, a lawyer and an Oxford scholar. Trade is represented by a merchant and a shipman. There are a number of burgesses: a haberdasher, a carpenter, a weaver, a dyer, a tapestry-maker, and their cook, as well as the Wife of Bath. Among the rural dwellers are a miller, a reeve, a maniple and a plowman.

With the only exception of the parson who is rather favourably represented, practically all those connected with the church are drawn either with touches of irony and subtle satire or with open repugnance. The worst among them are the pardoner and the summoner, both of whom not only have the most repulsive physical appearances but are possessed of a most odious character and inveterately indulge in cheating and oppressing the common people. The friar is scarcely any better, being a wanton and jolly fellow who instead of caring for the poor and the sick as he should, frequents places of merriment and cheats the poorest widow out of her last penny by giving her penance. In portraying the religious persons of higher rank Chaucer resorts to subtle irony rather than open ridicule. The monk is shown to love hunting and a fat roasted swan, things strictly forbidden to those who join the monastic orders. The prioress is painted as a most affected woman who aspires all the time to ape gentility.

Another striking phenomenon concerning a number of the pilgrims is their common practice of acquiring money by improper means, often by downright cheating and trickery. Both the lawyer and the doctor make use of their professional knowledge to make money, the former from the legal deeds he handles and the latter out of astrology and the pestilence. The miller, the reeve and the manciple pile up their wealth by tricking and fooling their betters in social station. The miller knows well how to steal corn; the reeve cunningly lends to his master what is the latter's by right; the manciple can fool all the thirty learned gentlemen he serves.

Yet another striking reflection of the social reality of the day is the growing feeling of self-importance shared by all the burgesses. The haberdasher, the carpenter, the weaver, the dyer and the tapestry-maker, are all well-to-do handicrafts men and well-clad, and rich and discreet enough to be aldermen and their wives like to be called madam and have precedence in church services and guild festivals. Even the wife of Bath who is somewhat deaf and gap-toothed likes to wear heavy and gaudy clothes and would get angry if some other woman in the parish tries to precede her while making an offering in church.

Other pilgrims are also objects of Chaucer's ridicule or humour. The merchant is so cunning that no one knows he is in debt. The Oxford scholar has a ludicrous appearance of being lean and threadbare and an inactive bookworm. Even the young squire appears ludicrous for being so much in love that he sleeps no more than a nightingale.

However, Chaucer had his respect for the two landed gentlemen in the company, the franklin and especially the knight who is called "a true, perfect, gentle knight". On the other hand, the poet's eulogy for the parson and the plowman is also rather significant, as it has been suggested that this might have been due to the influence upon the poet of the Lollardy and the peasants' rising of 1381.

The twenty-four tales narrated are of unequal merits. Taken as a whole they represent practically the whole range of literary genres in medieval and early Renaissance Europe, embracing minstrelsy, chivalric romances, fabliaux, lays, legends, legendary epic sagas, animal epics, mythology, moral allegories and sermons. Though Chuacer did not always succeed in his experiments with all the different popular literary media of the day, he certainly had wide interest in numerous literary traditions and innovations not alone in England but also on the Continent of Europe.

Of particular interest to us are those tales that contain rather keen social criticism. The three tales by the three ugliest figures among the ecclesiastical pilgrims — the pardoner, the summoner and the friar — together with the portraits of these three pilgrims in the General Prologue, produce strong impressions upon the readers of the depths of moral degradation to which the members of the three branches of religious profession could sink. Not only does the pardoner's tale of three rioters murdering one another for the possession of a pile of golden florins reveal the consuming passion for money in the feudal-bourgeois society of Chaucer's day, but the use of the very tale by its narrator the pardoner to lead up to his comments on the prevalent sin of avarice and thence to the need of all the pilgrims present to buy pardons and the saints' relics from him is a thorough-going exposé of the most tricky and unscrupulous pardoners of the age and a penetrating satire on the gullible and superstitious crowd falling for the papal pardons "hot from Rome" and for all sorts of fake relics of the saints. The friar's tale of a greedy summoner trying to extort money out of a poor widow and the summoner's tale of a hypocritical and avaricious friar attempting to squeeze dry the sick, bedridden Thomas are companion pieces that not only serve as pungent lampoons on the impious, rapacious summoners and friars in medieval England, but the two tales, together with the terrific feud and mud-throwing between the summoner and the friar as two fellow pilgrims that appear in the "links" preceding and following the two tales, are obviously meant by Chaucer to indicate the sharp intramural conflict between two different branches of ecclesiastical professions. The fact that Chaucer and his two fellow poets Langland and Gower concurred in their ridicule and censure of most of the ecclesiastics is surely no coincidence but a very definite reflection of the moral degeneracy common to the clericals at the time. Of Chaucer's other tales mention should be made of the physician's tale, the prioress' tale and the canon yeoman's tale, in which slander and religious persecution and cheating are objects of censure. In the physician's tale, the judge Appius' slanderous accusation of the virtuous Virginia led to the innocent girl's death but also the deserved punishment for the judge and his accomplice Claudius. In the prioress' tale, the religious persecution even resulted in the terrible murder of a helpless Christian child. In the canon yeoman's tale, cheating with the practice of alchemy as carried on by a canon is exposed, and this serves only as a rebuke on the medieval superstitious belief in the converting of baser metals into gold. Chaucer's parody on certain literary practices of his time may also be detected in two of his tales. In the monk's tale, one dull "tragedy" is related after another until the narration is called a halt to by the host of the inn serving as guide, who likewise puts a stop to Chaucer's own long-winded tale of Sir Thopas. In these two tales we may see the poet's disparagement of some long dull tragic stories and certain tiresome chivalric romances that he must have come across in his reading.

A group of three tales — the wife of Bath's tale of an Arthurian knight, the Oxford clerk's tale of the patient Griselda and the franklin's tale of Arveragus and Dorigen — have been well known as "the marriage group", because they all have to do with the problem of marriage, or rather with the question of whether the husband or the wife should be the dominating person in marital relationship. The wife of Bath's tale illustrates the view that what women most desire is mastery over their husbands and that therefore only the wife's domination can lead to peace and happiness in a household. The Oxford clerk's tale points to the attainment of happiness by a woman acting in full submission to her husband, suggesting thereby that the wife's patience and meekness is the key to married bliss. The franklin's tale recounts the ultimate happy ending of a married couple who overcome their dangers in life with mutual trust and understanding and seems thus to recommend the middle path of reciprocal love instead of mastery one way or the other. These three tales together, plus the striking image of the wife of Bath, a well-to-do and independent woman of a skilled clothmaker who has had five husbands and other lovers besides, reflect the rising social status of city-bred women in Chaucer's day as well as the poet's interest in the woman's position in the family.

Though an overwhelming majority of the tales in the collection are borrowed from or at least suggested by some source-book or other,

Chaucer in each case recasts the story and makes each tale suit well the profession and character of its narrator. So the knight tells a tale of chivalric romance about two knights and cousins Palamon and Arcite falling in love with the same young lady and about their ensuing contest with each other, while his son the lovesick squire relates an Oriental romance about Cambuscan. These two tales, together with the man of law's romance of domestic love that narrates the vicissitudes of the guiltless and unfortunate Constance, testify to the poet's indebtedness to the different types of romances of current popularity. The prioress and the second nun are made to tell respectively the legend of St. Mary and the pious Christian boy and the story of St. Cecilia, while the parson preaches a long, drawn-out sermon in prose. Also, true to their character, the miller, the reeve, the shipman and the merchant all tell uproarious but rather coarse ribald stories about husbands duped by their wives, stories of cuckoldry and illicit love drawn from the fabliaux of the Middle Ages but also comparable to some products of early Renaissance literature such as may be found in Boccaccio's "Decameron". Likewise, it is quite natural for the manciple and the nun's priest to tell tales drawn from the animal-epics or bestiaries, respectively about the white crew of Phoebus and concerning the chanticleer and the fox.

Though here and there we may find some tales very dull and long-winded, such as the parson's sermon and Chaucer's own tale of Melibeus, most of the tales as well as the prologues and links that go with some of them are not infrequactly filled with humour and irony, or even calling for uproarious laughter. But Chaucer's ever-present humour is manifest above all in his character-portraits of the different pilgrims, revealed chiefly in the general prologue but reinforced in many cases in the tales told and in the accompanying prologues and links. The interplay between the pilgrims, highlighting frequently the prologues to the tales and the links, and showing the rivalry or antagonism between centain pairs of pilgrims is particularly interesting, as these passages show the author writing with his tongue in his cheek and trying all the time to provoke a wry smile or open laughter from the readers. Even in depicting thoroughly disgusting and detestable figures like the pardoner and the summoner and the friar or despicable persons of hypocrisy and greed like the man of law, the physician, the miller, the reeve and the manciple, Chaucer displays his humour and irony as he condemns these vicious characters and their culpable deeds. This all-pervading humour mixed with satire constitutes Chaucer's high artistic achievement in "The Canterbury Tales" and enables him to tower above his contemporaries as a poet and a teller of tales.

Chaucer is also a great master of the English language. It has generally been conceded by literary historians that in his hand the London dialect of his day was crystallized into an effective weapon for satire and humour and for poetry. In "The Canterbury Tales" Chaucer's language becomes a most supple means of communication. With it he not only could at one moment be quite serious and at another be light-hearted and full of fun but he was able to produce at will truly poetic passages or lapse into a very intimate conversational style to suit an easy-going narrator of familiar stories. And the heroic couplet was employed in the poem with true ease and charm for the first time in the history of English literature.

"The Canterbury Tales" as the crowning glory of Chaucer's poetic career elevates the poet to the almost unquestioned foremost position among the host of poets and raconteurs in the whole period of Middle English literature.

SECTION III   ENGLISH LITERATURE OF
THE FIFTEENTH CENTURY.

1.   The Background: Political and Social.

The fifteenth century marked the definite decline of feudalism and the rapid growth of capitalist relations in trade and industry, as Britain went through a period of transition from the medieval to the Renaissance world. The peasants' rising of 1381 and a series of minor risings in subsequent years, the rise in wages and the fall in agricultural prices resulting in the disappearance of serfdom and the rise of a powerful yeomanry, the agitation among the small priests against the corruption and extravagances in the monasteries and among the higher ecclesiastics — all these factors led inevitably to the further decay of feudal relations and the feudal mode of production in early fifteenth century. In the meantime, the weaving industry grew rapidly in the villages and the suburbs of towns and fulling mills began to be set up in new centres higher up in the valleys where a better water - power was available. Many of the older towns went into decay while new centres of production sprang up and became towns with flourishing trade and industry.

The Hundred Years' War entered its second phase as Henry V resumed the hostilities with France and won a spectacular victory at Agincourt in 1415. But the emergence of Jeanne d'Arc in France and disunity and strategical errors on the English side eventually lost for England all the gained French territory except Calais, and the crushing defeat at Chatillon in 1453 ended the century-long war.

Inside England reaction toward heavy taxation and oppression culminated in the Lollard rising led by Sir John Oldcastle in 1418 and then in Jack Cade's rising of peasants and small landowners and part of the London plebeians in 1450. The nobles organized armed retainers drawn from unemployed soldiers and made armed raids and counter-raids on their neighbouring estates. The deposition of Richard II in 1399 and the accession of Henry IV led to subsequent struggles among the bigger nobles for the crown, and this strife for state power culminated in the War of the Roses in 1455 - 1485 which ended in the bloody annihilation of most of the big feudal barons and the final termination of their feudal rule throughout the country. The accession of Henry VII in 1485 began the period of Tudor monarchy with strong central authority but dependent upon merchants and other elements of the bourgeoisie for cooperation and support.

The military strife between England and Scotland in the 13th and 14th centuries, when Scottish forces led by William Wallace and then by Robert Bruce struggled for national independence from the English invaders under Edward I, Edward II and Edward III, was followed by a general lull in the 15th century, and a sort of permanent but irregular warfare on a small scale developed on the English-Scottish border.

Literate population grew with the rapid development of trade and industry in the towns and the break-up of feudal relations in the countryside, and in the middle of the 15th century the introduction of the printing press into England by William Caxton led to rapid growth in culture throughout the country. In the field of literature, folk literature, especially folk ballads, became an important feature in the 15th century.

The decline of the chivalric romance found its swan-song as a literary genre in Sir Thomas Malory's "Le Morte d'Arthur", a sort of summing-up of the Arthurian legend. Theatrical activities flourished and out of the sacred drama that had grown up for some time in the Christian churches, developed a secular drama, with secularized mystery and miracle plays and moralities performed by the town guilds. The influence of Chaucer was keenly felt among the poets both in England and in Scotland in the 15th century, and these writers were known as the English and Scottish Chaucerians. The literature of the 15th century was in a transitional stage between the two periods of great literary flowerings in England in the 14th and the 16th centuries.

2. The English and Scottish Popular Ballads: "Robin Hood Ballads".

The English and Scottish popular ballads flourished particularly in the 15th century, though the earliest of them, extant, dated back to the 13th century and the later ones belonged to the 16th and even the 17th centuries. Most of them were sung and circulated and then written down in the 15th century but they were not collected nor published till much later. The best known of the earliest publications of these ballads was that by Bishop Thomas Percy of the second half of the 18th century, in his "Reliques of Ancient English Poetry". After that other collections were published, and imitations of these ballads were written, especially by the romantic poets of the early 19th century like Coleridge and Keats. The most extensive collection of these ballads was made by Professor F.J. Child in his 5-volume "English and Scottish

Popular Ballads", published in 1882 – 98, in which there were a total of 305 ballads collected, the greatest number of them belonging to the 15th century.

These popular ballads constitute one of the main streams of English literature in the 15th century when there were no great poets comparable to Chaucer of the 14th century or to Shakespeare and Marlowe and Spenser and Sidney of the late 16th century. They were essentially people's literature, composed by the people and for the people. They were generally narrative poems that originated in oral form, not unlike the epics of classical and medieval times though very much shorter, and were written down only after they had passed on from mouth to mouth for some length of time. A number of them were originally sung or chanted or could be sung and chanted, and some were connected with folk dances (the word "ballad" came from the French word "baller" meaning "to dance"), while most of them had a choral, dramatic presentation. Though they usually had a collective or communal origin, yet whether they were composed by individual authors or by groups of people at dances and other folk gatherings is uncertain, most likely the case varying with different ballads. Certainly these ballads are simple poems that reflect the social life essentially from the point of view of the common people, though not infrequently they tell stories about the king and the nobility and sometimes even represent the sentiments and thoughts of the feudal ruling class or the rising bourgeoisie in the cities. These ballads of the 15th century were chiefly English but also partly Scottish, a number of them narrating incidents on the English-Scottish border and known as "Border Ballads". By far the most significant group of these ballads is the series of 37 ballads of different lengths in Child's collection, that deal with the famous outlaw Robin Hood and his men and their activities. Considered by some critics as the "most extraordinary ballad cycle", these poems, by describing the legendary figure of Robin Hood and his followers and their exploits, not only reflected the fleeing of English peasants to the forests in the 12th, 13th and 14th centuries to avoid feudal oppression but also depicted the activities of the organized armed outlawry by these peasants against their chief oppressors the sheriffs, the bishops, the abbots and the barons and revealed these outlaws' desire to help the poor and right the wrongs and above all to live a life of quietness free from tyranny. And though the stories about Robin Hood and his fellow outlaws were told also in other works like Robin Hood plays and romances, and in vague and brief mentions in historical or semi-historical records, it is chiefly in these ballads that the legend about Robin Hood as a heroic figure lives and is preserved for posterity.

Possibly the longest of the Robin Hood ballads, entitled "A Gest of Robin Hode", contains eight "fyttes" and 456 stanzas in which three threads of the outlaw's story are strung together, plus an epilogue on Robin Hood's death. The first thread tells how Robin helps a poor knight to pay his debt to an abbot by robbing a monk of the abbey. The second thread relates how Robin with the help of his faithful follower Little John captures their chief enemy the sheriff of Nottingham and eventually kills him. The third thread narrates a series of encounters between Robin and the king coming to arrest him and ends in the king pardoning Robin and the latter finally running away back to the greenwood. The final episode is a brief sketch of Robin treacherously betrayed and killed by a wicked prioress and her lover. Though here are traces of the poet's illusion about the king and a poor knight, yet the ballad reveals clearly that these peasant outlaws' chief concern was to help the poor and oppressed and to punish the oppressors. Near the beginning of the poem Robin Hood in a reply to Little John declares the general policy of the outlaws: to do no harm to husbandmen and yeomen and knights and squires who are good fellows but to deal harshly with bishops and archbishops and chiefly the high sheriff of Nottingham. In a number of other ballads about Robin Hood there is also the mention of the sheriff of Nottingham as the chief enemy, possibly because the latter was chiefly responsible for most of the direct assaults upon the outlaws in their greenwood forest.

Another longer ballad about Robin Hood, entitled "A True Tale of Robin Hood", was written in the strict "ballad metre" and contains a rather complete narrative of Robin Hood's adventures from his early days to his death, and it was the work of a known author (Martin Parker) in 1632. Here, while the poet tries to show that Robin Hood was born a member of nobility and only later became an outlaw after having consumed his wealth, there are however some very succinct statements about Robin Hood as one who hates and robs the abbots and the bishops and the monks and the friars and all the miserly rich and is ever ready to help the widow and the fatherless and all the poor men in distress and suffering from famine. Toward the end of the ballad, a sort of summing-up of all the exploits of Robin Hood and his men is given in one stanza:

"Full thirteen yeares, and something more,
    These outlawes lived thus,
Feared of the rich, loved of the poore,
    A thing most marvelous."

A large group of these Robin Hood ballads deal with Robin and his men in their struggle against the oppressors of one kind or another. Some treat of the eventual killing of a sheriff or a monk ("Robin Hood and Guy of Gisborne" and "Robin Hood and the Monk") or of the punishment of the oppressors, usually a sheriff or a bishop, by depriving them of money or goods ("Robin Hood and the Potter", "Robin Hood and the Butcher", "Robin Hood and the Bishop", "Robin Hood and the Bishop of Herefore" and "Robin Hood's Golden Prize"). Others tell of the rescue of innocent persons from unjust punishment by the oppressors ("Robin Hood Rescuing Three Squires", "Robin Hood Rescuing Will Stutly" and "Robin Hood and the Beggar") or the frustration of the oppressors to trap the outlaws ("Robin Hood and the Golden Arrow"). Two devices commonly employed in these struggles against oppression are the use of collective force through the blowing of a horn (by Robin himself or by Little John) to summon a large number of other armed outlaws to assist in the fight, and the playing of some ingenious trick upon the oppressors by means of disguise (Robin Hood all the time in disguise, occasionally even as an old woman, as in "Robin Hood and the Bishop"). These are among the most forceful and most typical of the Robin Hood ballads.

Quite a number of these ballads deal with Robin and also with his men engaged in single encounters of hard combats with different individuals who later would be reconciled to them or even join their group of outlaws in Sherwood Forest. In these ballads the fight and the later reconciliation often become a convention, a formula with little meaning attached to them. A few shorter ballads have to do with Robin Hood's relations with the king (Richard I) and Queen Katherine. Most of these end in reconciliation between the outlaw and the monarch. Only one ("Robin Hood and the Valiant Knight") shows Robin and his men refusing to surrender but fighting to the last with Sir William and his soldiers sent by the king to quell the outlaws, and the poem ends with Robin becoming ill and then treacherously murdered after returning to the greenwood. Occasionally we come across a light and delightful piece describing the outlaws' assistance lent to lovers for their happy union ("Robin Hood and Allen A Dale"). And there are also ballads about Maid Marian whom Robin loved and married and with whom he lived in content, and also about Little John as one of Robin's chief lieutenants.

Taken together, the ballads on Robin Hood are important specimens of English literary heritage because in them perhaps more than in other literary works of the 15th century are truly reflected the hopes and fears and the loves and hates as well as the illusions of common English people at the time, and the fascination of their poetic form born of simplicity and dramatic intensity has endeared them to countless readers since their time.

Next to the Robin Hood ballads in fame and importance are the "Border Ballads", dealing with bloody battles fought on the border of England and Scotland. Among them the two best known are "The Hunting of the Cheviot" (otherwise called "Chevy Chase") and "The Battle of Otterburn", both probably referring to the same fight between Percy of Northumberland in northern England and Douglas of Scotland, though with different endings to the story. In "The Battle of Otterburn", the Earl of Douglas led a Scottish force to attack the castle of Otterburn in Northumberland and was surprised in their camp by Henry Hotspur, Lord Percy, and the result was Douglas killed and Percy taken prisoner. In "The Hunting of the Cheviot", there was family feud on top of the national quarrel between England and Scotland. Percy hunted for three days across the Scottish border in his spite of Douglas, and as a result a fierce battle took place between the two sides, with many people slaughtered including both Percy and Douglas. In the former poem only Douglas was killed while Percy was merely taken prisoner, but in the latter ballad both warriors were slain. Another difference is that in the former poem Douglas and his Scottish force appear to be the aggressors, while in the latter the blame of the battle seems to be placed upon Percy's haughtiness and his hot challenge against Douglas. This suggests that one ballad was possibly written from the English point of view whereas the other from the Scottish stand. However, in both ballads the wholesale slaughter on the battlefield was much bewailed (obviously the common people's viewpoint) though the chief actors Percy and Douglas who were directly responsible for the slaughter, were shown to be heroes wilful and cruel yet courageous and honourable, this last apparently partly due to the influence of feudal, chivalric way of thought upon folk literature. "The Hunting of the Cheviot" or "Chevy Chase" has been especially highly praised by the 16th-century poet Philip Sydney and then by the 18th-century critic and journalist Joseph Addison.

Some few ballads are based on the Arthurian legend or biblical material. Of the former there is one entitled "The Marriage of Sir Gawain", the theme of which bears close resemblance to that of the well-known 14th century romance "Sir Gawain and the Green Knight" — the theme of a knight of chivalry true to his promise (in this particular case specifically the promise to meet his enemy on New Year's Day) and loyal to his leader or king. "Dives and Lazarus", a typical ballad drawn from the story of the rich man and the leper in the Bible, is significant in the realistic pictures given of the relations between the rich and the poor, of Dives feasting and Lazarus starving and begging at his door and being treated with whips and biting dogs. Though here is the conventional religious ending of Lazarus eventually rising to heaven and Dives entering hell and repenting after his death, the suggestion of social injustice is unmistakable from the contrasting pictures of luxury and misery in the earlier stanzas.

Perhaps the commonest themes in the English and Scottish popular ballads of the 15th century are those having to do with domestic life, particularly with the relations between different members of a family or between lovers. Usually the relations represented are unnatural ones, including murder and treachery and ending generally in tragedy. For instance, "Edward" is about the murder of father by son, "The Twa Sisters" about that of sister by sister, "The Cruel Brother" of sister by brother, "The Twa Brothers" of brother by brother, and "Lord Randal" of a lover by his faithless mistress. Some of these stories are about lords and ladies while others seem to be about the common people, but in all of them the obvious tone is that of condemnation of the criminals perpetrating their crimes.

Numerous ballads treat of the theme of love. The nominal heroes and heroines in them may often be lords and ladies, but generally there are no echoes of the romantic and unrealistic relations of knights and ladies in the chivalric romances. What we find here are rather the poignant emotions of love and hate and faith and treachery that belong to the city plebeians and the peasant folk of the time. "Child Waters" is an example of a story about a woman's constancy in love, a sort of Griselda story in which a patient woman with steadfast love for her lover is made to endure such cruel tests of love as were permissible only in the feudal world of man's unquestioned supremacy over woman. A better known ballad on the same theme is "The Nut-Brown Maid". There are also ballads on the theme of faithlessness and treachery in love ending in tragedy ("Fair Margaret and Sweet William", "Lord Thomas and Fair Annet", etc.) or love-tragedies resulting from sheer mischance (e.g., "Lord Lovel").

Superstition not infrequently plays an important part in the ballads: a magic diamond ring in "Hind Horn", a fantastic visit to the elfland in the well-known "Thomas Rhymer", and frank ghost lore in "Sweet William's Ghost" and "The Wife of Usher's Well". The last of these tells a most moving tale of three sons getting drowned on a voyage but returning every night as ghosts to visit their mother who believes them to be still alive. In spite of such superstitious belief as the necessity for the ghosts to depart before cock-crow, the poem contains a very vivid picture of a simple woman's true maternal grief for the loss of her sons.

There are some few ballads on political treachery, among which the best known is "Sir Patrick Spens". This is a Scottish tale in which one of the best sailors, Sir Patrick Spens, was the object of treachery when some elderly knight suggested that the king send him on a most perilous voyage in stormy winter weather. Sir Patrick knew the grave danger of the errand but as an obedient subject to the king he took up the assigned task and eventually got drowned. With an obvious note of censure on the treachery, the poem succeeds in telling a touching story of the unhappy fate of an old sailor and obedient subject.

There are also ballads showing the spirit of revolt toward oppression of one kind or another. In "Captain Car, or Edom of Gordon", the courageous lady of the castle defies the threats of the traitor Captain Car and is even ready to risk her own life and the lives of her own children by steadfastly refusing to submit to the ruffian's orders. In "Lamkin", stronger defiance comes from one of the labouring folk against his unjust employer who is a member of the nobility. Here a mason named Lamkin builds a castle for Lord Wearie but receives no payment from him, so he plots with the nurse of the lord's household and kills the lady of the castle and her baby, but the lord returns and both the mason and the nurse are condemned to death. The defiant words of the nurse to the mason when the latter asks her to bring a basin to hold the blood of the lady because she comes of noble kin are meaningful utterances of the common folk against the unnatural social distinction between the nobility and the poor people:

> "What better is the heart's blood
> O' the rich or the poor?"

There are a few ballads that provide striking instances of the intelligence and ingenuity of the common labouring people. In "King

John and the Bishop", when the king threatened the Bishop of Canterbury with death unless the latter could answer his three questions
satisfactorily, it was a shepherd who had the ingenuity to answer the
questions cleverly on behalf of the bishop and thus saved the latter's life.
In "The Crafty Farmer", when an old peasant met a gentleman-thief
on the way, he not only kept safe the forty pounds of money he had
with him but was clever enough to fool the rogue and get hold of the
latter's portmanteau containing 300 pounds of silver and 300 pounds
of gold. Though both ballads chiefly aim at humour and though the
ingenuity of the shepherd and the peasant is revealed merely in their
employment of little tricks, here at least is shown how the seemingly
simple-minded labouring folk are not without native sagacity to help
themselves and others out of difficulties and especially against knavery
or oppression. Alongside of these there is another ballad, "Get Up
and Bar the Door", in which in the description of a little tiff between
a peasant and his wife is shown ample humour of the simple people.
In the winter when the wind was blowing north and south, "our good
wife" and "our good man" had an argument about which of whom
should "go out and bar the door" and they agreed between them that
the one who spoke the first word should "bar the door". Then two
gentlemen came at night and they ate the puddings on the stove and in
order to make the man and wife speak, one of them threatened to
shave off the good man's beard with boiling water and the other to kiss
the good wife, and upon that "our good man" spoke angrily and "our
good wife" followed up with

> " 'Good man, you've spoken the foremost word,
>   Get up and bar the door.' "

Though here we find only slight touches of humour, yet the presentation of simple incidents in the simple life of simple people in
simple language makes the poem a valuable document on "the
annals of the poor".

Most of the popular ballads are short and so, generally speaking,
they deal only with brief incidents, usually in a succession of brief scenes,
or are mere fragments of longer tales. Often a ballad is full of gaps

and omissions, with some of the actions briefly sketched or merely hinted at, and the reader has the feeling of plunging abruptly into a situation as if beginning with the last act of a play. Therefore the success of a ballad depends very much on the art of drawing with a few strokes a vigorous sketch of events and situations, and the better ballads are usually dramatic and exciting, with suspense and climax, and capable of producing the effect either of deep pathos or great joy, through bitter irony or subtle humour. There is generally much dialogue in a ballad, frequently involving sudden shifts from narrative to dialogue. Not infrequently do we find in the ballads elaborations and even repetitions, or sometimes the practice of repeating a stanza with slight modifications that advance the story. The language is on the whole rather simple with little play of fancy in the use of epithets or in the arrangement of words and phrases.

The ballads appear in different verse forms. The older ballads sometimes employ 2 – line stanzas, in couplets, followed by a burden or refrain. The common form of later ballads, known as the ballad metre, contains 4 – line stanzas, with the alternation of 4 – and 3 – feet verse to the odd- and even-numbered lines (sometimes all four lines are in octosyllabics, each with 4 feet of iambic verse), and rhyming usually on the second and fourth lines. Refrains are sometimes used, though not often. The ballad metre, sometimes rigidly followed though more often loosely employed, has frequently been adopted by later poets as verse form for short narrative poems or merely as vehicle for personal lyrics.

3. Early English Drama: Folk Drama; The Mystery Plays; The Miracle Plays; The Morality Plays.

Early English drama consisted of folk drama and church drama. The early germs of folk drama lay in the sword dance and the morris dance. The sword dance was a sort of pantomimic dance, symbolizing the primitive idea of the expulsion of Death or winter and introducing as its chief character the fool in fox's skin. The morris dancers were also known as the ploughboy dancers, their dramatic performance taking place generally on Plough Monday which marked the resumption of agricultural work in early spring. The performance was that of the regular grotesque figures of village festivals, including the fool and the hobby horse, amid much dancing and rimed speeches, or that of some character killed and brought back to life. These dramatic elements developed into the mummers' plays or St. George plays, in which the hero, usually St. George, King George or Prince George, kills or is killed by his opponent, and then a doctor, usually a comic figure, restores the dead man to life, true to the theme of resurrection in the earlier plays. Often an episode of a dragon conquered by St. George would be introduced, and the original pagan story is generally Christianized with the appearance of such characters as Father Christmas and Beelzebub. And there were comic characters and much dancing and music. None of these plays were written down till as late as the 18th or even 19th century. There were also a number of Robin Hood plays that resemble the Robin Hood ballads, in character and theme and even in details of story. They were written down in the 15th and 16th centuries.

Ironically enough, while the Roman Catholic Church in the days of the Roman Empire forbade the performance of secular drama on the grounds of its immorality, it was inside the church that the early germs of drama sprang up in the late Middle Ages and later developed into various types of church drama which in turn developed eventually into secular drama. As early as the 9th or 10th century, in the liturgy or religious service inside the Catholic Church, in England as well as in France and other European countries, there were elements from which church drama evolved. In high mass on great commemoration days and high festivals, there were chants alternating between the priest and the congregation or the choir representing the congregation, together with recitative passages, plastic decorations and representations, solemn processions as well as the ritual of movement and gesture. Such performances have been known as liturgical dramas because they were part of the liturgy or religious worship, and the most important part or the nucleus of this liturgical drama was the tropes, or dialogued chants between the priest and the choir representing the congregation. These tropes and the recitative passages were at first all in Latin. One of the earliest tropes in England preserved today dates back to about A.D. 900.

Gradually these tropes were enlarged and the whole performance for the representation of episodes from the Bible became more lively and more realistic. In the course of time this dramatic representation became no more a part of the religious service, and was first moved from the choir of the church to the nave inside the church, and then to the churchyard and eventually to the village greens, the market-places and the streets. And the purpose of these performances changed from a spectacle for the edification of the congregation to entertainment for the public, accompanied by the change in the language used, from Latin to English, and by the dropping of choral singing and other musical elements in favour of the spoken dialogue. The acting roles at first borne by the clergy were also gradually taken up by lay actors. The short episodes of drama based on passages from the Bible became more fully developed and lengthened and were linked together to form more continuous stories. In this way the early liturgical dramas gradually passed into the cycles of mystery plays and miracle plays.

In France the Mystery Plays were rather sharply distinguished from the Miracle Plays, but in England the two terms were used almost interchangeably, though strictly speaking the former refer to dramas based directly on stories from the Bible whereas the latter deal with the legends of the Christian saints. The Mystery or Miracle Plays in England were written in cycles, consisting of a whole series of plays covering the biblical narrative from the creation of the world through the life and passion of Christ down to the Last Judgment. These cycles were formed soon after the beginning of the 14th century though a goodly number of the individual plays must have been written in the 13th century or even earlier.

These cycles of Mystery or Miracle Plays were staged by different trade-guilds in different towns, with individual plays assigned to appropriate guilds. These plays were produced on "pageants", each of which consisted of two storeys, with the upper storey serving as stage and the lower one as dressing-room for the players, and in the towns the pageant was movable and could be wheeled about from street to street and would generally halt at busy market-places or street corners to give performances. In the country, a long series of immovable scaffolding remained fixed at one place and the audience moved about to see one play after another. Cycles of mystery plays seem to have existed only in some of the larger towns. There are only four cycles extant that are more or less complete in the presentation of the whole biblical story: the York cycle with 48 plays, the Towneley or Wakefield cycle with 38, the Chester cycle with 25, and the Coventry cycle, also known as the "Ludus Coventriae", with 42. The other cycles preserved in other towns are fragmentary if at all. Miracle plays in the strict sense of the term, or plays on the lives of the Christian saints, were never popular in England and few of them are extant.

The best known mystery play in England is the so-called "Second Shepherds' Play", or the second of the plays on the shepherds, in the Towneley or Wakefield Cycle. As the play opens, the three shepherds who are later to greet the newborn Christ come onto the stage one after another and complain of their sufferings in cold stormy weather, homeless and poor and heavily taxed and oppressed by their masters the gentry who live in great comfort and luxury. Then Mak the sheep-stealer enters and steals a sheep after pretending to sleep together with the shepherds. Mak takes the stolen sheep home and hides it in a cradle. The shepherds go to Mak's home to search for their lost sheep, and by accident one of them finds the sheep in the cradle. They then punish the thief by tossing him on a blanket. And after this rather lengthy comic episode the play ends with the main theme or the raison d'etre of the drama when the shepherds go to pay their respects to the new born Saviour at the manger. The great significance of this play lies in the creation of the entirely uncalled-for comic episode of sheep-stealing and more importantly in the strong social criticism latent in the shepherds' complaints of their sufferings at the hands of their masters. It is also interesting to note here how the seeds of secular drama are sown in such an ostensibly religious play.

These mystery and miracle plays were all written in verse, usually in rather complicated stanzas and often with both rhyme and alliteration.

The Morality Plays or Moralities sprang up in England in the 15th century alongside of the Mystery and Miracle plays. They are different in that they do not tell stories from the Bible nor about the lives of the saints, but as products of the age of allegories they employed abstractions, such as virtues and vices, to serve as characters in order to illustrate certain moral or religious doctrines in abstract form. The best known of the Morality Plays is "Everyman", produced in the last quarter of the 15th century. The play deals with what is supposed to happen to Everyman toward the close of his life. God sends Death to summon Everyman and the latter looks about for some one to accompany him and to plead for him before God. Many personified characters appear one after another, but the upshot of the story is that while all his good friends Fellowship, Kindred and Goods as well as the common virtues Beauty, Strength, Discretion and the Five Wits cannot help him, only Good Deeds whom Everyman has long abandoned is able to plead for him and save him at the side of the grave. The moral lesson conveyed by all these personified abstractions in the play is of little interest to us today, and the only saving feature of the "Morality" for the modern reader consists in the few scenes of Fellowship, Kindred and Goods showing great regard for Everyman at first and later forsaking him completely. Here we may find some fine pictures of the hypocritical and pharisaical feudal-bourgeois society of 15th-century England.

The Morality Play, different from the Mystery and Miracle Plays, gives the author more freedom to invent his stories instead of having to follow more or less the biblical tales or the legends about the saints. And the use of personified abstractions leads naturally to the creation of character-types, especially the well-known character of "Vice", a sort of a fool or buffoon, a companion to the Devil, to assist the latter in his business or to wrangle with him and mock him, thus providing fun and comedy.

As Morality Plays flourished in the 15th century and continued into the 16th, a new species, the Interludes, emerged. Two Morality Plays in the 16th century were written by two prominent writers: "Magnificence" (c. 1516) by the poet John Skelton and "Pleasant Satire of the Three Estates" (1540) by the Scottish writer David Lyndsay.

4. The English Chaucerians; Early Scottish Poetry and the Scottish Chaucerians.

Chaucer's influence was very strongly felt in the 15th century, both in England and in Scotland. On the whole the Scottish Chaucerians are greater poets than their English counterparts.

The chief figure among the English Chaucerians is John Lydgate (c. 1370 – c. 1450) who has been known as "the monk of Bury" because he was a monk of the Suffolk Abbey of Bury St. Edmunds for the greater part of his life. Possibly personally acquainted with Chaucer, Lydgate called the latter his "mayster" in his poems. Very popular in his day and known as the most voluminous poet of the age, he has met with rather adverse criticism since the age of the Renaissance, and his major poems ("Troy Book", "The Story of Thebes", "The Falls of Princes" and "The Temple of Glass") have been blamed for heaviness and long-windedness in story-telling, for flatness of diction and enormous verbosity and for the very irregular metre and totally unscannable verse. Only in a few of his shorter poems, notably in the lively little piece "London Lickpenny", which tells of the misadventures of a penniless country-fellow in London shops and streets, are to be found some admirable touches of humour in the vivid descriptions of persons and scenes in the English capital.

A little earlier than the Scottish Chaucerians were two Scottish poems of patriotism that deserve mention: Barbour's "Bruce" and Henry the minstrel's "Wallace", both celebrating national heroes of Scotland.

"The Bruce" (1375) by John Barbour (? 1316 – 1395) has generally been considered as the earliest important literary work written in the

Scottish (or the Scots) dialect by a Scottish writer. For more than thirty years the archdeacon of Aberdeen and in his later life one of the auditors of the exchequer, Barbour probably studied at one time at Oxford and then in France.

"The Bruce", sometimes considered an epic but actually a curious combination of romance and historical poem, sings of the Scottish people's struggle for national independence from their English aggressors under the heroic leadership of Robert the Bruce. Beginning with the hero's daring act of slaying a traitor at the foot of the altar in a sanctuary, the poem proceeds with the Bruce's adventures hiding in the mountains and making narrow escapes from the traps set for him and fleeing to the small island of Rachin, and ends when the national leader with his band of warriors wins a great victory at Bannockburn over Edward II of England and secures the independence of Scotland. The whole tale is told with much vigour and vividness and strong patriotic fervour, and Bruce's affection for the common people is well illustrated in the poem when the hero in disguise seeks for his lodging among the country folk and when he delays the march of his army so as not to leave behind to the mercy of the Irish savages a poor laundress who is at the time too ill to be moved. The rather lengthy description of the battle of Bannockburn serves as the natural dramatic climax in the whole story and reveals not alone the poet's high patriotic fervour but also his masterful dramatic and descriptive power. But the true highlight in the piece is the deservedly celebrated passage on freedom which has been considered one of the most lyrical utterances on freedom in all English and Scottish peotry:

"A! Fredome is a noble thing!
Fredome mays man to haiff liking!
Fredome all solace to man giffis,
He levys at ese that frely levys!
A noble hart may haiff nane ese,
Na ellys nocht that may him plese,
Gyff fredome fail; for fre liking
Is yarnyt our all othir thing.

Na he that ay has levyt fre
May nocht knaw weill the propyrté,
The angyr, na the wretchyt dome
That is couplyt to fould thyrldome.
Bot gyff he had assayit it,
Than all perquer he suld it wyt;
And suld think fredome mar to prise
Than all the gold in warld that is."

Directly in the tradition of Barbour's "Bruce" but written almost a century later was the "Wallace" of Henry the Minstrel, commonly called Blind Harry, a wandering minstrel, blind by birth and earning his food and clothing by the recitation of his poems in the halls of the great. "Wallace" (c. 1460) deals with the life and adventures of William Wallace (?1272 – 1305), a Scottish patriot who led the Scottish people to resist the English aggressors but was finally captured as a result of treachery and executed in London. Not so much a historical poem as a traditional romance, "Wallace" nevertheless enjoyed even greater popularity than Barbour's "Bruce", though artistically it is marred by some very obvious exaggerations in the descriptions of the battle and of the prowess of the hero.

Four Scottish poets of some repute in the 15th century were all Chaucerians: James I of Scotland, Robert Henryson, William Dunbar and Gavin Douglas.

King James I of Scotland (1394 – 1437) was captured by an English ship at the age of 11 and was kept prisoner at Windsor for 19 years. During the last year of his captivity he saw from the windows of his prison Lady Jane Beaufort, daughter of the Earl of Somerset, and fell in love with her at first sight. She returned his love and they were married in 1424. In the same year he was ransomed and returned to Scotland and was crowned there. He ruled for 13 years and then was assassinated. He is now chiefly known for his one great poem, "The Kingis Quair" ("The King's Book") (1423 – 4), written in the form of a medieval allegory but recording the poet's personal experience in love. The poem was composed in the rime royal and under Chaucer's influence, with many of the incidents drawn freely from the latter's "The Knight's Tale".

Robert Henryson (?1425 – ?1500) was schoolmaster at the Benedictine Abbey grammar school in Dunfermline and was probably at one time a member of the University of Glasgow. His best known work is "The Testament of Cresseid", admittedly a continuation of Chaucer's "Troylus and Criseyde". In this sequel to Chaucer's poem, Cresseid is shown to be cast off by Diomede after he is satiated with her. She takes refuge with her father Calchas, but one day she reproaches Venus and Cupid and is punished by them and becomes a leper. She begs by the wayside and is met by Troylus who passes riding by. The two cannot recognize each other but Troylus gives her rich alms because she reminds him of Cresseid, and the girl learns later who he is. Before she dies she makes a testament bidding a fellow-leper take her ruby ring to Troylus who recognizes the ring and in his great sorrow orders a tomb to be built for Cresseid. The poem was written by Henryson obviously with a moral aim: that the tragic ending is the only fitting close to the life of a wanton woman like Cresseid. The verse form used, like that in Chaucer's "Troylus and Criseyde", is also the rime royal and the poetic style is likewise in definite imitation of Chaucer.

William Dunbar (?1460 – ?1520) went to the University of St. Andrews and then for a time was a Franciscan friar, leading the life of a wandering preacher. Later he went to France, probably on a diplomatic mission and fell under the influence of the French society and of the French poet François Villon. By 1500 he was back in Scotland as a priest at the court, pensioned by the king and moving about as a minor official in royal business. From then on he became a court poet, pouring forth a constant stream of ballads, complimentary verses, satires, burlesques and humorous addresses to the king.

In spite of his fame as the chief among the Scottish poets of his age, Dunbar shows little originality in his numerous writings. Most of his longer poems are conventional allegories, with the employment at times of alliterative verse. Of his shorter pieces three satirical poems may be mentioned: "Tidings from the Session" as an attack on the lawcourts, "Satire on Edinburgh" as a denunciation of the filthy conditions of the Scottish capital, and "Black Lady" containing a covert hit at the courtly craze for tourneys. But the most outstanding of Dunbar's briefer pieces and indeed of all his poems is his "Lament for the Makaris" ("makaris" means makers or poets). Suggestive of the works of the French poet François Villon and containing an effective Latin refrain "Timor mortis conturbat me" ("The fear of death disturbs me"), the poem bewails the transitoriness of human existence and mourns the inevitable passing away of all persons of different stations and professions, enumerating particularly the deaths of the poets in England and Scotland (beginning with Chaucer). Written with touching solemnity and in short stanzas it is a gem of an elegy.

Gavin (or Gawain) Douglas (c. 1474 – c. 1522), an earl's son and bishop, received his education at the University of St. Andrews. He then took orders and after rapid promotion became dean or provost of the collegiate church of St. Giles in Edinburgh, in 1501. Between that year and 1513 was done all his literary work, including his magnum opus, the translation of Virgil's "Aeneid". After that he was deeply involved in politics and in 1516 was appointed to the bishopric of Dunkeld. He died of the plague in London in 1322.

Douglas' chief claim to fame lies in his translation of "The Aeneid", the first English translation of the whole of the ancient Roman classic in 10 – syllable riming couplets. He also prefixed each of the 12 books of Virgil's epic with a prologue, his original contribution. Especially important are the prologues to the 7th, 12th and 13th books (the 13th book being the work of Mapheus Vegius, not of Virgil) in which are given vivid pictures of winter and the months of May and June, anticipating James Thomson's "Seasons" of the 18th century.

5. **English Prose of the 15th Century: Sir Thomas Malory and his "Le Morte d'Arthur".**

Sir Thomas Malory's "Le Morte d'Arthur" is the only monumental work of prose in 15th-century England. Recent research tends to identify Malory with the son of a Warwickshire gentleman who possibly participated in the Hundred Years' War, then was knighted before 1442 and became Member of Parliament in 1445. He later fought on the side of the House of Lancaster in the War of the Roses, then was accused and found guilty of criminal acts and was imprisoned for a number of years in the Newgate Prison. He probably wrote "Le Morte d'Arthur" while in prison and probably died there 1471. "Le Morte d'Arthur" was completed in 1469, and was published first by William Caxton in 1485, possibly with certain revisions by Caxton.

Malory's "Le Morte d'Arthur" is a kind of final summing-up of the Arthurian legend built up from the 12th to the 15th century, though it does not contain all the stories about King Arthur and all his knights. In the 21 books that make up the romance, Malory linked up the various threads of the legend centering round the birth, the exploits and the death of King Arthur, including the stories about Merlin, about Arthur's queen Guenevere, about his knights of the Round Table (chiefly Sir Launcelot, Sir Tristram, Sir Gawain, Sir Galahad, Sir Percival, Sir Balin, Sir Gareth, Sir Palomedes and the traitor knight Sir Mordred) and about the quest for the Sangrael (i.e., the Holy Grail). The main things narrated have to do with the wars and tournaments and all sorts of knightly adventures (including the quest of the Sangrael which was engaged in by almost all the knights of the Round Table and is touched upon in seven of the 21 books), but there are also long passages on love intrigues, (in most cases illicit love such as Sir Launcelot's love for Queen Guenevene and Sir Tristram's for La Belle Isoud, wife of King Mark of Ireland), and there are descriptions of deeds of treachery (i.e., of Sir Mordred and of Morgan le Fay, Arthur's sister).

More specifically, the first five books of the romance deal principally with King Arthur (except for a large part of Book II devoted to Sir Balin), beginning with descriptions of his father Pendragon and the magician Merlin who serves as his protector in his youth, and then proceeding with Arthur's marriage to Queen Guenevere and the formation of the knights of the Round Table and ending with his war against the Roman Emperor Lucius and with his subsequent exploits in Almaine and Italy and against the Saracens. The three books VI-VIII deal each with one outstanding knight and his adventures: with Sir Launcelot (Book VI), Sir Beaumains (or Sir Gareth) (Book VII) and Sir Tristram (Book VIII). Books IX-X describe several long tournaments (one of them lasting to the third day and another lasting to the seventh) and adventures of several of the Arthurian knights including Sir Launcelot and Sir Tristram. Books XI-XVII have to do chiefly with the quest of the Sangrael by almost all the Arthurian knights, particularly Sir Percival and Sir Galahad, with the latter eventually partaking of the Sangrael and becoming king. Books XVIII-XIX concentrate on the guilty love between Sir Launcelot and Queen Guenevere which has been touched upon many times already in the preceding books but which here reaches its climax when the queen, twice accused of treason, is at first successfully defended by Sir Launcelot but later gets into trouble the second time, with the knight caught in a trap and imprisoned (though he escapes later). Books XX-XXI wind up the romance with the narration chiefly of Sir Mordred's treachery and rebellion against King Arthur and then the death of both Mordred and Arthur after a battle, while the relations between Arthur and Launcelot (first their reconciliation over Guenevere and then war between them again) as well as the ultimate fate of Guenevere and Launcelot (she becoming a nun and he a monk) are also touched upon.

A 16th-century Puritan scholar and prose writer Roger Ascham spoke strongly against Malory's "Le Morte d'Arthur", accusing the romance of containing nothing but open slaughter of men and immoral love. In a way this is quite true. In the adventures of the knights and in the quest of the Sangrael, and especially in the wars and the long tournaments described in the romance, we not only witness extreme cruelty and barbarism practised under the high-sounding appellation of chivalry, but we may also see quite clearly the absolutely meaningless practice of fighting and killing simply for the sake of fighting and killing and for nothing else. This is so especially in the case of the interminably long tournaments or jousts where so many brave knights are slain or maimed for life. On the other hand, though treachery (of Mordred and Morgan le Fay) is generally condemned, illicit love is not so but is sometimes even eulogized as part of true knightly conduct, so much so that Guenevere instead of feeling guilty for her betrayal of Arthur rather blames Launcelot severely for his unfaithfulness to her in his relations with Elaine, whereas in the case of Tristram and La Belle Isoud the two young lovers are somewhat excused for their misbehaviour and even sympathized with, on the ground of their innocence and of their having drunk the love potion. And Malory the author, being a knight himself and having taken part in the cruel and blood-thirsty War of the Roses, obviously upheld these bloody traditions of feudal knights and their adventures and tournaments and illicit love affairs, and wrote his romance in their defence and with gusto.

"Le Morte d'Arthur" may well be called the swan-song of feudal knighthood and chivalry which were much idealized in the heyday of feudalism. The Arthurian romance also at one time served as literary vehicle for the eulogy of knightly deeds and virtues as we find in the 14th-century "Sir Gawain the Green Knight". But with the late Middle Ages passing gradually into the early Renaissance, further laudatory writings on knighthood and chivalry became something decadent and even retrograde because they suggested looking backward rather than forward. However, in spite of the undeniable fact that Malory meant his romance to be a sort of an elegy mourning the passing of the age of feudal knighthood and chivalry, the objective effect of this realistic rather than idealized presentation of the Arthurian legend is an unmistakable though unintended exposé not alone of the barbarism, hypocrisy, treachery and immorality of the supposedly brave and heroic knights and their beautiful ladies, but also of the thoroughly unreal and fantastic pictures of feudal grandees in meeting with all sorts of strange superstitious situations and performing ridiculous and unbelievable deeds.

"Le Morte d'Arthur" is an important landmark in the development of English prose from late Middle English to early modern English, and has the distinction of being written in a lucid and simple style. Both the Arthurian legendary material it contains and its facile prose style had their wide and lasting influence upon English literature of later centuries.

Chapter III

ENGLISH LITERATURE OF THE RENAISSANCE

SECTION I   THE HISTORICAL BACKGROUND: ECONOMIC, POLITICAL AND CULTURAL.

1.   The Renaissance in Europe.

The Renaissance as an epoch of social and cultural development embraced all Western Europe.   On the foundations of medieval society and culture the Renaissance first rose in Italy in the 14th century and came to a flowering in the 15th and then in the 16th century it spread to other countries, notably France, and thence to Germany and England and Spain and the Low Countries (i.e.,   Holland and Belgium). About the chief characteristics of this epoch Engels wrote in his introduction to the "Dialectics of Nature":

"Modern natural science, which alone has achieved an all-round systematic and scientific development, dates, like all more recent history, from that mighty epoch which we Germans term the Reformation, ... and which the French term the Renaissance and the Italians the Cinquecento. ... It is the epoch which had its rise in the last half of the 15th century.   Royalty, with the support of the burghers of the towns, broke the power of the feudal nobility and established the great monarchies, based essentially on nationality, within which the modern European nations and modern bourgeois society came to development. And while the burghers and nobles were still fighting one another, the peasant war in Germany pointed prophetically to future class struggles, not only by bringing on to the stage the peasants in revolt — that was no longer anything new — but behind them the beginning of the modern proletariat, with the red flag in their hands and the demand for common ownership of goods on their lips. In the manuscripts saved from the fall of Byzantium, in the antique statutes dug out of the ruins of Rome, a new world was revealed to the astonished West, that of ancient Greece; the ghosts of the Middle Ages vanished before its shining forms; Italy rose to an undreamt-of flowering of art, which seemed like a reflection of classical antiquity and was never attained again. In Italy, France and Germany a new literature arose, the first modern literature; shortly afterwards came the classical epochs of English and Spanish literature. The bounds òf the old orbis terrarum were pierced. Only now for the first time was the world really discovered and the basis laid for subsequent world trade and the transition from handicraft to manufacture, which in its turn formed the starting point for modern large industry. The dictatorship of the church over men's minds was shattered; it was directly cast off by the majority of the Germanic peoples, who adopted Protestantism, while among the Latins a cheerful spirit of free thought, taken over from the Arabs and nourished by the newly discovered Greek philosophy, took root more and more and prepared the way for the materialism of the 18th century."

Here from Engels' analysis we may see the chief characteristics of the Renaissance: (1) politically the feudal nobility lost their power and with the establishment of the great monarchies there was the centralization of power necessary for the development of the bourgeoisie; (2) the Catholic Church was either substituted by Protestantism as a result of the so-called Reformation (as in Germany and England) or weakened in its dictatorship over men's minds (as in Italy and France and Spain); (3) geographical discoveries opened up colonial expansion and trade routes to distant parts of the world and brought back gold and silver and other wealth and also broadened men's mental horizons; (4) in the countryside the peasants were terribly exploited and they either rose in uprisings or ran away and flocked to the cities and added to the proletariat there; (5) in the cities the merchants and the master artisans grew in wealth and in power and became the bourgeoisie while handicraft turned gradually into manufacture and the modern proletariat sprang up among the employed workers in the factories; and finally,

(6) culturally, as the interest in God and in the life after death was transformed into the exaltation of man and an absorption in earthly life and as materialistic philosophy and scientific thought gradually replaced the church dogmas and religious mysticism of the Middle Ages, a totally new culture rose out of the revival of the old culture of ancient Greece and Rome and out of the emergence of a new philosophy and science and art and literature through the exploration of the infinite capabilities of man.

These characteristics may be found in the era of the Renaissance in all western European countries, with minor differences in their diverse political and economic and cultural environments. In literature, in the 14th and 15th centuries, in Italy, we have such big names as Petrarch, Boccaccio, Ariosto and Tasso, and in the 16th century in France there were Rabelais and the Pléiade and Montaigne, in Germany von Hutten and Martin Luther, in Holland Erasmus, in Spain Cervantes, and in England Thomas More and Marlowe and Shakespeare. These progressive writers, sometimes known as humanists, at their best voiced the human aspirations for freedom and equality and against the tyranny of feudal rule and ecclesiastical domination, and in their various ways they attacked the civil wars and welcomed the centralized rule of monarchs, sang the praises of geographical and scientific discoveries and explorations and with them the trade expansions and the amassing of wealth from abroad, condemned political oppression and religious dogmatism and persecution and satirized the numerous social vices of money-worship and cheating and dissipation and hypocrisy of all sorts. In their literary and philosophical works some of these humanists went back to the ancients—the ancient Greek and Roman writers and philosophers—for their inspiration and followed the latter in their views for life on earth as against life after death and in their materialistic philosophy as against religious fanaticism and superstition. These humanists chiefly stood for the progressive thought of the rising bourgeoisie together with their inevitable bourgeois limitations.

In the field of English literature though the influence of the Renaissance in Italy was already felt in the last part of the 14th century when

Chaucer already learned from the great Italian writers Petrarch and Boccaccio, yet Chaucer was still essentially a medieval writer and 14th-century England was still in the later stages of the Middle Ages, economically and politically. The Renaissance, as a social and cultural epoch, did not arrive in England till the last part of the 15th century and the early years of the 16th. The War of the Roses which came as the last of the baronial wars in 1455 – 1485 not only thoroughly weakened feudalism but actually killed off most of the feudal nobility in England whose existence in the past had been responsible chiefly for the feudal division and strife that prevented the centralization of political power so essential for the full development of a bourgeois society. Henry VII (1485–1509) and Henry VIII (1509–1547) laid the foundations of a strong monarchy. Another social event of great importance was the intensification of economic exploitation of the peasants including the large-scale enclosure of common land to be used for pasturage, which led to the peasants' and plebeians' uprisings of Jack Cade in 1450 and of Robert Kett in 1549 and to the wholesale eviction of peasants from the countryside who were thereby hurled onto the labour-market in the cities as free plebeians. A third major historical landmark was the Reformation which in England took the form of the establishment of the Anglican Church and the disavowing of the authority of the Pope in Rome. This last led to the stoppage of the papal revenues in the form of monopolies and especially to the confiscation of the lands and properties of the monasteries which in turn led to the creation by the king of a new aristocracy with land estates and to the expropriation of the tenants on the land and of the inmates of the monasteries. Though there was a brief period of counter-reformation during the bloody reign of Mary Tudor (1553 – 1558), yet except for those few years the Church of England with the English monarch as its head was maintained ever after Henry VIII's Act of Supremacy in 1531. These three major events in the domestic affairs of England—the end of feudal division resulting in the expropriation of the noble men's retinue, the expropriation of the peasants from the countryside and the confiscation of the monasteries—plus the geographical exploration and trade expansion and the spoliation of gold and other treasures from abroad, constituted what Marx called the "primitive accumulation of capital" which paved the way for the establishment of the capitalist relations in replacement of the feudal social system. And the result was the growth of the cities, the development of a capitalist textile industry and a big overseas trade, and the parliament representing the interests chiefly of the bourgeoisie co-operated well with the centralized monarchical rule, with minor reservations and conflicts.

More strictly in the literary field, the so-called revival of learning, including chiefly the study of the ancient Greek language and the growing interest in classical Greek and Roman literature and philosophy, came into being in England in the last years of the 15th century and especially in the early days of the 16th, with Oxford University as the centre of these activities. Also, because the Renaissance as a cultural movement began in Italy and spread to England via France, Italian and French literatures of the 14th, 15th and 16th centuries became popular in England and were much studied and imitated. The Reformation brought with it the attacks on church dogmas and superstition and the satires on the clerical profession, especially on the personnel of the Catholic Church including the monks, the friars, the pardoners, the summoners, etc., and earthly bliss was voiced as against sheer otherworldliness and asceticism while science and materialistic philosophy tended to oust religious mysticism and fanaticism. There was the growing interest in man and in the infinite capabilities of man as against implicit faith in God. And with such a literary and philosophical background, English literature of the Renaissance flourished and surpassed that of the Middle Ages that preceded it, not alone in scope and variety but also in the high quality of its achievement, in the long period of its flowering and in the great number of its great writers and their great works.

2. Stages and Trends of English Literature of the Renaissance.

English literature of the Renaissance may be conveniently divided into three stages of development, and the two chief literary trends run-

ning through the three distinct stages are on the one hand court literature mainly representing the interests of the monarch and the old and
new aristocracy and on the other hand bourgeois literature reflecting
chiefly the thoughts and feelings of the rising bourgeoisie and to a lesser
extent also of the small plebeians. The three stages are: (1) from the
last years of the 15th century to the first half of the 16th, from the introduction of the first printing press in England by William Caxton in
1476 through the group of the so-called "Oxford Reformers" down to
the prose of Thomas More (especially his "Utopia") and the poetry of
Skelton and Wyatt and Surrey and the later church dramas such as the
moralities of David Lindsay and the interludes of John Heywood; (2)
the so-called "Elizabethan Age" (1558 – 1603), covering roughly the
second half of the 16th century, but especially the last two decades:
(a) in poetry, from the influence of Wyatt and Surrey in "Tottel's Miscellany" in 1557, through the sonnets and longer poetical works, but
chiefly lyrical poetry, of Sidney and Spenser to Shakespeare and Ben
Jonson and John Donne; (b) in drama, from the influences of church
drama and folk drama and ancient classical drama through the University Wits, chiefly Lyly, Greene, Kyd and Marlowe, to the more mature comedies and the early tragedies of Shakespeare; (c) in prose fiction,
from Lyly's "Euphues" and the prose romances of Sidney and Lodge
and Greene to the "picaresque" "Unfortunate Traveller" of Nashe
and the more realistic narratives of Deloney's about city plebeians and
labouring people; (3) the first quarter of the 17th century or the Jacobean period (James I's reign 1603 – 1625): (a) in drama, from the great
tragedies of Shakespeare's to his later tragi-comedies and from the
comedies of humours of Ben Jonson's and the tragi-comedies of
Beaumont and Fletcher, through the "blood-and-thunder" plays of
Webster and Ford and the realistic dramas of Dekker, Middleton,
Thomas Heywood and Massinger, to the decadent comedies of James
Shirley; (b) in poetry, from Ben Jonson and Donne to their followers and
the imitators of Spenser; (c) in prose, from the essays and the scientific
and utopian writings of Francis Bacon and the King James Bible of
1611 to the pseudo-scientific "Anatomy of Melancholy" by Robert

Burton.

SECTION II ENGLISH LITERATURE OF THE EARLY 16TH CENTURY.

1. "The Oxford Reformers"; Thomas More.

The so-called "Oxford Reformers" and Thomas More have sometimes been called "humanists" in certain literary histories, to refer specifically to the revival of the culture or the humanities of ancient Greece and Rome that took place in England in the last years of the 15th century and the early decades of the 16th.

The "Oxford Reformers" include chiefly William Grocyn (1446 – 1519), Thomas Linacre (1460 – 1524) and John Colet (1467 – 1519), all three of whom were students and then teachers at Oxford University, travelled and studied in Italy and introduced the study of ancient Greek as well as the new science and philosophy of the time in opposition to the rigid church dogmas of medieval scholasticism. The eldest of the three, Grocyn, came into contact with Italian literature of the Renaissance during his visits in that country and returned to England to become the first teacher of ancient Greek language and culture at Oxford, having among his students Linacre and Thomas More and also the famous Dutch humanist Erasmus. Linacre went to Italy with the English embassy and stayed there for over ten years and contacted many Italian humanists there and studied medicine. After his return to England he taught Greek at Oxford besides serving as physician and Greek grammarian and translator and together with Grocyn made Oxford famous internationally as a centre of Greek studies. Colet, son of a London mayor, and student of Grocyn and Linacre, travelled in France and Italy and met many Italian humanists and, upon his return, became Lecturer on the Greek New Testament at Oxford, then was Dean of St. Paul's Cathedral in London (1505) and founded the famous St. Paul's School, a sort of a model secondary school, where he tried to introduce reforms to the educational system of the day by emphasizing the study of Greek and Latin and secular science. Here mention should be made of Desiderius Erasmus (1465 – 1536), the great Dutch humanist of the time, who being dissatisfied with his education at Paris and too poor to go to Italy made several visits to England and studied at Oxford under Grocyn and became a great friend of Thomas More. Though he was a Dutch scholar, his works in Latin had their influence in England, and especially the book "Encomium Moriae" (1511) which was later (in 1549) translated into English as "The Praise of Folly" and which contained piercing satires on medieval scholasticism became one of the most widely read books in England of the time.

In early 16th century Oxford University became the first important centre of ancient classical culture in England, and these "Oxford Reformers" helped to spread the light of new science and new world outlook and combat medieval scholasticism and thus laid the foundations for the rise of a new literature in England in the later decades of the 16th century. Their contributions to English literature of the Renaissance should not be overlooked even without including among them the much greater figure of Thomas More and his great work "Utopia".

Thomas More (1478 – 1535) was the son of Sir John More, a judge, and received his education at Oxford where he was the pupil of Grocyn and Linacre. For a time in his youth he was a page at the household of Cardinal Morton who had been a leading politician during the War of the Roses. His father made him study law and he became a well-known lawyer but he kept up his interest in literature and maintained intimate relations with the Oxford humanists Colet and William Lily and also Erasmus. In 1504, when he was only 22, he entered parliament, but his career as an M.P. was cut short after he offended Henry VII by speaking in the parliament against the king's demands for subsidies. For a time he entered a monastery, but his knowledge gained there of the dissipation and ignorance and hypocrisy of the monks made monastic life repulsive to him and he returned to secular life. For some time he remained in obscurity in order to avoid the punishment and wrath of Henry VII. When Henry VIII came to the throne in 1509, More returned to active social life and in 1510 became an under-sheriff of London and in 1514 was Master of Requests. In 1515 he was sent to the Low Countries to negotiate a commercial treaty, and it was during this mission that he first conceived and wrote the second part of his famous book "Utopia", and then completed the first part in the following year (1516) when the whole book, in Latin, was published in Louvain.

Soon More was given one important political post after another. In 1518 he was privy councillor; in 1521 he was government treasurer; in 1525 he was chancellor to the Duchy of Lancaster; in 1528 he was Speaker in the parliament; and in 1529 he replaced Cardinal Wolsey as Lord Chancellor, a post equivalent to that of prime minister. Previous to this, More had helped Henry VIII in controversial writings against Martin Luther the leader of the Reformation in Germany and in 1528 he completed his "Dialogue", his first controversial book in English which was directed mainly at William Tyndale, one of the earliest translators of the Bible into English. In 1531 Henry VIII, ostensibly on account of the papal refusal to grant his divorce from Queen Catherine (of Aragon) but also for his desire to stop papal monopolies and take over rich church estates and monasteries for himself, broke with the Pope in Rome and with the Catholic Church, and established the national Church of England (or Anglican Church), with himself as the head. More remained faithful to Catholicism and resigned his chancellorship in 1532. Though he was willing to swear fidelity to the new Act of Supremacy, he refused to take any oath rejecting the Pope's authority or admitting the justice of the king's divorce from Queen Catherine, and he was sent to the Tower of London for imprisonment. Then he was indicted of high treason and was found guilty and beheaded in 1535.

More's works included writings both in English and in Latin, but he has chiefly been remembered for his "Utopia" which became almost immediately popular following its first publication in Latin, and then was translated into English in 1551 by Ralph Robinson and then into French, German, Italian and Spanish. "Utopia" was written in 1515 when, according to the author's own account at the beginning of the first part of the book, he met a friend of his, Peter Giles, at Antwerp, who introduced to him a sailor named Raphael Hythloday, and then the three of them had a conversation together. Then Hythloday the humanist-traveller tells of the conditions in England and in the second part there is a description of the ideal country of Utopia (a Latin word meaning "nowhere") in the midst of an unknown sea. While the first part is more or less a realistic reflection of the English society of More's own age, the second part is under the influence on the one hand of the then recent maritime discoveries of the Portuguese and the Spaniards in their explorations boyond the Atlantic Ocean, especially of Amerigo Vespucci, and on the other hand of the "Republic" of Plato.

In part I, social evils in early 16th-century England are exposed and attacked. First, there are described the severe laws for hanging the thieves, laws with which More as a lawyer was only too familiar. Then the sources for the innumerable thieves ("twenty criminals could often be seen hanging from a gallows in a row") are analyzed and traced. The wounded soldiers returning from the many foreign wars and dismissed from the army as well as the retainers dismissed from noblemen's services on account of their sickness became thieves and robbers. Then, above all there are the enclosures of land, the evictions of small tenants and the lessened demand for workers on the land, because rich landlords find grazing farms more profitable. So More revealed the miseries of the masses in England, and pointed out that "even a beast's life seems enviable" as compared with that of a labourer. On the other hand, the feudal lords were described as leading the lives of the drones that did no work but enjoy the luxuries created by others. And he summed up by describing the society as "a conspiracy of the rich against the poor."

Part II is even more significant; it is a valuable document of utopian socialism. And it is very well linked up with part I. At the end of the first part we are told that the cause of all the social evils in England is the existence of private property, and in the second part More points out that the abolition of private property is the foundation of the ideal society.

In Utopia, all land is held in common and there is no private property of any kind. All citizens must take turns to work on the farms in the countryside for a few years. Things needed in daily life may be obtained at the store-houses, for the consumption of goods is organized by the state, as is also the production of goods. Every one, except for the leaders chosen for the government and scholars or philosophers, must engage in physical labour, but the hours of work each day are limited to six. The rest of the time is spent in going to lectures and amusements. Here the principles underlying this picture of an ideal society resemble to a certain extent those of scientific socialism, but here the private ownership of all things, and not just that of the means of production, is abolished.

In Utopia, all the citizens, men and women, are on an equal footing and have the same rights. The magistrates, high and low, are all elected on a democratic basis: the prince and tranibors being elected by syphogrants who are in turn elected by heads of the households, and a household of kinsfolk is the smallest social unit for production and for livelihood and consumption. Here there is the trace of the author's yearning for the patriarchal mode of existence in the pre-feudal age.

In Utopia there is also universal education for all children, male and female, and education is conducted strictly on the basis of rationalism, by means of reasoning and persuasion instead of corporal punishment.

In More's ideal commonwealth, therefore, there is no private ownership, no idleness, no exploitation, and there is democratic rule, there is socialization of production as well as socialization of distribution, and there is rationalism. In all these respects, and in the author's disbelief in the possibility of an enlightened monarch and in his condemnation of the all-powerful money, More went further than the other humanists of the Renaissance not only in England but in all Europe.

In the land of Utopia, there is, however, the existence of religion, though people may have freedom of belief or worship. Gold and silver are no longer considered as valuable, but are artificially turned into objects of contempt, to be regarded as children's toys and chains for prisoners. War is held in contempt and is only permitted in self-defence, and foreign mercenaries are to be employed to serve as cannonfodder. Wives are subject to their husbands and prisoners of war and offenders of law are made into slaves who are deprived of civic rights and forced to endure hard labour. In these respects we see More's limitations, particularly in the existence of slaves and in the inequality between wives and husbands, showing respectively the influence of Plato and of the ancient Greek slave society, and of the belief in male supremacy in the feudal world. But here, at the same time, the spirit of the author's age, that of the Renaissance and the Reformation, is fully reflected, especially in his views on religious toleration, against the waging of wars and against the worship of gold. Also, we may see More's opposition to asceticism as he exalts material happiness as the aim of life and emphasizes the gratification of one's physical senses as well as of one's mind and intellect.

In More's "Utopia", therefore, we may see the ruthless exposé of the cruelty of the English ruling classes in their oppression and exploitation of the peasants and a rather vivid picture of a utopian socialist state, but writing at the dawn of capitalism, More could not but build his dream of a communist society on the social foundations of handicrafts manufacture, and this limitation of his age when there were yet no big industries nor a ripened proletariat, necessarily made his conception of an oppressionless, exploitationless society a rather vague, dreamy world which did not have its sound political, economic and social bases. And More's limitations as a member of the ruling and exploiting class himself manifest themselves in his indifferent attitude toward slaves and mercenary soldiers and in his actual contempt for physical labour — in spite of his insistence on the need of most utopians to participate in physical labour. Finally, when we compare More's views in "Utopia" with his life as a courtier and especially as a fervent Catholic who chose rather to die than to give up his belief in the absolute authority of the Pope in Rome, we find curious but unmistakable contradictions in his world outlook.

2. Court Poetry: Skelton; Wyatt and Surrey.

From the last years of the 15th century to the first decades of the 16th, the chief English poets include John Skelton and Wyatt and Surrey. All three of them were court poets, but Skelton, being only a member of the upper petty-bourgeoisie turned courtier, was closer to the common people and could see more clearly the vices at the court and among the clergy and satirize them, whereas Wyatt and Surrey were both top-notch aristocrats and so their poetry was more representative of the thoughts and feelings of the nobility and its contribution to English literature lies chiefly in the innovations they made in verse form.

John Skelton (1460? – 1529), born in the middle of the 15th century, has sometimes been considered one of the last medieval English poets, but actually all his important poems were written in the first decades of the 16th century and he not only won praise from Erasmus and was a Latin grammarian and an Oxford laureate on account of his Latin verses, but was also a satirist on the vices of the court and of the clergy as well as an innovator of native English verse metre and style, so that he was rather more a Renaissance writer than a medieval poet.

Skelton went to Cambridge University where he took the degree of M.A. in 1484. In 1490 he was elected laureate at Oxford, and later also at Cambridge and Louvain University, and became a protégé of Henry VII. In 1498 he took orders and then was tutor to the future Henry VIII. In 1504 he became rector of Diss in Norfolk. Later he went to London where he at first received favours from Henry VIII and was a friend of Cardinal Wolsey but afterwards wrote several verse satires against Wolsey and had to take refuge in the sanctuary of Westminster until his death in 1529.

Skelton's first important poem was "The Bowge of Court" (1509?) (the word 'Bowge' is a corrupt form of the French word 'bouche', meaning court-rations or free board at the king's table), which is an allegorical satire on the life at the court of Henry VII. The allegory describes how the young poet Dread goes on a voyage to the land of Favour on board a magnificent ship, how on the way he meets with several of Fortune's friends, Favell (or Flattery), Suspecte (or Suspicion), Disdain and Dissimulation, who conspire against him, and how he is about to throw himself into the sea in order to avoid the troublesome company when he awakes and finds himself in a dream all along. The allegorical figures and fantastic descriptions were all employed by Skelton to ridicule the moral degeneracy among the courtiers, and, instead of following the Italian verse forms here as was the fashion in early 16th-century England, Skelton used the native English stanza of seven heroic lines, after Chaucer.

Three other well known poems of Skelton's are: "The Book of Colin Clout" (1519 – 24), "Speak, Parrot" (1517 – 18) and "Why Come Ye Not to Court?" (1522 – 23), all of which contained attacks on Cardinal Wolsey, especially on the evil consequences of the latter's domination. Colin Clout, as a peasant who resembles Langland's Piers the Plowman, is a prominent figure in these poems, where the clergy, instead of acting as good shepherds to the people who were compared to flocks of sheep, were described as shearing all the wool off the sheep and praying for nothing but their own profit and advancement. And his attack on the clergy of the Catholic Church was chiefly aimed at Wolsey who acted then as the head of the Catholic Church. Here we also find the most often quoted lines from Skelton as the poet speaks of his own verse:

> "For though my rime be ragged,
> Tattered and jagged,
> Rudely rain-beaten,
> Rusty and moth-eaten;
> If ye take well therewith,
> It hath in it some pith."

The "pith" takes the form of sharp satire while the ragged rime is the characteristic form of "Skeltonic verse" which consists of short lines frequently of two or three feet each (occasionally even of one foot) and which contains quick recurring rhymes in a rapid movement of verse. Though this Skeltonic metre was sometimes called "doggerel", it is actually a very effective vehicle for Skelton's biting satire and vigorous humour.

Two other outstanding poems by Skelton are: "The Book of Philip Sparrow" (1503 – 07) and "The Tunning of Elynour Rumming". The first is an elegy, containing first a lamentation from the mouth of a young woman Jane Scroupe over her sparrow killed by a cat, and then a eulogy of Jane by the poet and finally a defence of himself and the poem. Written as an echo to the famous 18-line lyric on a dead sparrow by the great ancient Roman poet Catullus, this typically Skeltonian poem of 1382 lines is a curious mixture of subtle humour and deep feelings, playful buffoonery and desultory mourning, also with sprinklings of satire on religious worship and knightly ideals and scholastic learning, in the poet's inimitable, rugged verse. "The Tunning of Elynour Rumming" is possibly the most remarkable poem by Skelton as it shows more clearly than any other work the poet's close kinship with the common people. Elynour Rumming is an alewife who dwells in the countryside and brews cheap ale for "travellers and tinkers, for sweaters and swinkers, and all good ale drinkers", and this rather long poem of seven "passus" or sections gives a realistic and humorous description of common country folk's simple enjoyment of ale-drinking in their moment of relaxation from toil, and the portraits of Elynour Rumming and her women customers are especially refreshing and lifelike.

Skelton's other works include: a "Ballad of the Scottish King" in which is celebrated the victory of Flodden for which the Scottish people won their freedom from England; a rather conventional morality play "Magnificence" in which a prince named Magnificence is brought to ruin by bad councillors but eventually saved by Good Hope and Perseverance and other virtues, but which contains certain attacks on the clergy and the court; "Garland of Laurel", also an allegorical poem in which the poet describes the crowning of himself among the great poets of the world; and "Ware the Hawk", a poem satirzing the clergy as being interested only in hunting and hawking and paying no attention to their duties toward the people.

Skelton was a great satirist with a most effective verse metre, a court poet whose chief virtue lies in his repeated attacks on the vices of the court and of the clergy.

Wyatt and Surrey have generally been mentioned together as rather outstanding landmarks in the historical development of English poetry, chiefly because their poems which appeared with prominence in the anthology known as "Tottel's Miscellany" in 1557 seemed to usher in a new period of flowering of lyrical poetry in England in the second half of the 16th century.

Sir Thomas Wyatt (1503 – 42) was born of an aristocratic family and was sent to Cambridge University at the early age of 12, graduating at 15 and taking his M.A. at 17. He made long sojourns in France and Italy and was therefore much under the influence of French and especially Italian literature of the Renaissance. Knighted in 1537, he did much diplomatic work as ambassador in Spain and in the Netherlands. He was imprisoned twice and in 1542 died on the way while engaged in a mission to meet the Spanish ambassador.

Wyatt wrote chiefly lyrics in different verse forms. His major contributions to English literature consist in his rather brilliant lyrics on the theme of love and in his introduction into English poetry the sonnet form from the Italian, and in both cases he was indebted to the great Italian humanist Petrarch whose "Sonnets to Laura" ("Sonnetti e Canzone in Vita ci Madonna Laura") had their tremendous influence all over Europe during the Renaissance. Wyatt's 30-odd sonnets mainly followed the Petrarchan sonnet in rhyme scheme, with minor differences,and adopted also the Italian poet's theme of a lover's entreaties to his mistress, and in both respects Wyatt set the pattern for many English poets after him in the second half of the 16th century. However, Wyatt's best-known poems were not sonnets but a few short love lyrics of shorter lines in different stanzaic forms such as: "Forget Not Yet", "My Lute, Awake", "And Will thou leave me thus?" Here Wyatt was also following the Petrarchan tradition of a lover's genuine passion for his unkind mistress but he introduced into his verse a song quality reminiscent of native English folk poetry of an earlier date. Though the theme employed was still that of courtly love between aristocratic ladies and gentlemen, yet the accent on earthly love between men and women marked a definite advance over the otherworldly chivalric love of medieval romances. In this way Wyatt's poems were unmistakably products of the Renaissance, and started a new tradition of love poetry in Elizabethan and Jacobean England. Besides, certain sentiments and expressions of native English folk lyrics of earlier centuries were absorbed along with a song quality, and this grew into a poetic tradition to be followed by manyEnglish poets of the late 16th and early 17th centuries, including Shakespeare and Ben Jonson and Sidney and the University Wits.

Another contribution of Wyatt's to English poetry was his introduction of other stanzaic forms from the Italian poets, such as Dante's terza rima (3-line stanzas rhyming aba bcb cdc ded ee) and Serafino's strambotti (octaves rhyming ababccc), to be used often by later English poets.

Henry Howard, Earl of Surrey (1517 – 1547), often known simply as Surrey, came from a higher aristocratic family than Wyatt: his grandfather and father were both dukes and from his early years up to manhood he was the companion of princes. Following the medieval tradition of chilvalry and knighthood he distinguished himself at the court for jousting with other courtiers and for versifying. He took part in the war with France, was wounded and appointed commander. Following the Petrarchan tradition he wrote many sonnets singing of his imaginary love for Geraldine (her real name being Elizabeth Fitzgerald) whom he had seen when she was only 12 and who was later married to an old man of 60. Upon the death of Wyatt who was 14 years his senior, Surrey wrote a poem "Of the Death of Sir T.W." When he was only 30, for quartering the royal arms he was accused of high treason by Henry VIII, convicted and beheaded.

Surrey's chief contributions to English literature were very much the same as those of Wyatt; they consist in his writing the first love lyrics in the English language in Petrarchan fashion and in his introduction of new verse forms into English poetry, particularly the English form of sonnet and the blank verse. Surrey's lyrics are slightly different from

Wyatt's, in that the younger poet employed more reasoning in the lover's entreaties to his mistress and used the sonnet and other lyrical forms also to write about friendship and other themes. But he has been chiefly remembered as the first poet to use the "English" sonnet form (with the rhyme scheme of ababcdcdefefgg instead of abbaabbacdecde) which was later adopted by Shakespeare and now known as the Shakespearean sonnet, and as the first English writer to employ blank verse in his translation from Latin of the second and fourth books of the great Roman poet Vergil's epic "The Aeneid".

Both Wyatt and Surrey died young and their poetry, except for some minor pieces, was published posthumously, in "Tottel's Miscellany" in 1557, so that the influence of their poetry was not felt till after the middle of the 16th century. But their contributions to the development of English poetry were valued highly by most critics, and their two names were frequently regarded as important landmarks ushering in the flowering of sonnets and lyric poetry of the Elizabethan age.

3. Morality Plays and Interludes of the 16th Century: David Lyndsay; John Heywood.

The morality plays, following in the tradition of mystery plays and miracles plays continued to enjoy great popularity in England in the 16th century. After Skelton's "Magnificence" (written about 1516), David Lyndsay, a Scottish poet and satirist, wrote a number of moralities of which the best known is "A Pleasant Satire of the Three Estates" in 1540, an extremely long verse-drama of 4630 lines that contains five units in all, three "interludes" of some length and two main parts of the morality. The play opens with the first main part of which there are two acts, with an interlude between. In Act I, Rex Humanitas (King Humanity) is tempted by Sensuality who introduces to him evil companions, and Good Counsel and Truth (Veritie) and Chastity were either expelled or put in the stocks. Then in the first of the interludes are told the several adventures of Chastity after her expulsion from the king, including her encounters with a tailor and a shoemaker and their wives which involve some rough horseplay. In Act II, Chastity is introduced to the king but objected to by Sensuality and is put in the stocks. Then Divine Correction arrives and the evil companions attendant on the king run away and Good Counsel and Truth and Chastity are set free from the stocks. Upon the advice of Correction the king consents to expel Sensuality. And the first main part of the play ends with the members of the parliament being summoned to appear at the court before the king.

Another interlude follows, and here the chief character Pauper, reduced to poverty by feudal and ecclesiastical oppression, is on his way to the king to seek for redress, but is driven out by the king's servant Diligence. Then Pauper relates to Diligence his miseries under the oppression and exploitation of his landlord and church dignitaries. He used to support his old father and mother by his labour and owned a mare and three cows. When his parents died the landlord took away the mare as a heriot (heriot being the money payment required for the landlord upon the death of a tenant), and the vicar seized the best cow at the father's death and the second at the mother's. The third cow was taken away when Pauper's wife died of grief, and the vicar's clerk took away the best clothes in the family. So now Pauper can do nothing but beg. The parish priest even refuses to let him take part in the communion service at Easter because he has failed to pay his tithes. He has only one farthing left in his pocket, and upon finishing his narration he dozes off. Then a pardoner comes and attacks the "wicked New Testament" and Martin Luther and speaks boastfully of the pardons and relics he comes to sell. After the pardoner has sold a dispensation to a shoemaker (soutar) for separation from his wife, Pauper wakes up and the pardoner begins to sell him a thousand years of pardon for the farthing Pauper still has with him. But when Pauper asks to see the indulgence he has bought and the pardoner has nothing to give him, a fight takes place and the relics all fall into the gutter. Though this is only one of the interludes in the drama, it is surely the most effective part of the play and tells in the most forceful way the tyranny and wiles of the ecclesiastics from which a poor farmer suffers from.

In the second main part of the play the three estates, the aristocracy

(Temporality or the Lords), the clergy (Spirituality) and the townspeople (Merchant or the representatives of the burghs), appear before the king in parliament, the three being led by different vices (Temporality by Public Oppression, Spirituality by Covetousness and Sensuality, and Merchant by Falsity and Deceit) Then Diligence summons all the oppressed to come and make their complaints before the king and John the Common Weal, representing the common people, delivers an impressive speech accusing the three estates of their evil-doings. Temporality and Merchant repent and promise amendment, but Spirituality remains impenitent as the abbot, the parson and the lady prioress seek to justify their violation of their religious vows. A long debate follows. Finally Correction comes and the abbot and the parson and the lady prioress are all punished and driven out to earn their honest living in secular occupations while the vices who come with the three estates are sent to the gallows. John the Common Weal takes his place in the parliament and acts for the reform of abuses are passed. The drama proper ends, but another farcical interlude follows, with a comic sermon delivered by a buffoon dressed up as Folly.

"A Pleasant Satire of the Three Estates" is one of the most important plays in the whole development of church drama in England, as it contains the author's piercing satire on the social evils of his time, with sharp attacks particularly upon the ecclesiastics. The play was written with much wit and in a clear style and shows the poet's easy command of rhymes. It is suffused with the spirit of the Reformation and the Renaissance as it attacks the vices within the Catholic Church and speaks for the miseries of the common people.

Existing at about the same time as the moralities, possibly a little later, are the interludes which are sometimes not so easily distinguishable from the moralities but which are on the whole more farcical and generally contain fewer or no allegorical figures. The chief writer of the interludes is John Heywood (1499 – 1580), who was born in London and spent his youth at the court of Henry VIII and participated in court presentations but who being a staunch Catholic suffered after Henry VIII broke with the Pope in Rome, and after a brief period of success during the bloody reign of Mary Tudor he emigrated to France after Queen Elizabeth's accession and died there.

John Heywood is known to have written altogether six interludes of which two are better known and more important: "The Play Called the Four PP" and "A Merry Play between Johan Johan the Husband, Tyb His Wife, and Sir Johan the Priest". While the second tells the story of a husband deceived and maltreated by his wife who carries on improper relations with a priest, the first is a satire on the ecclesiastics and the townspeople, with the "Four PP" (i.e., a Palmer, a Pardoner, a Pothecary (= apothecary) and a Pedlar) competing with one another over the telling of the biggest lie. Both interludes were written in the spirit of the Renaissance, and followed the tradition of the Italian humanist Boccaccio by writing against asceticism and by creating ridiculous portraits of church dignitaries such as the priest, the pardoner and the palmer. From the point of view of the historical development of drama in England, these interludes are important in that they broke away from the dull and allegorical church drama of the Middle Ages and heralded the native secular drama of the later decades of the 16th century.

SECTION III ENGLISH LITERATURE OF THE SECOND HALF OF THE 16TH CENTURY.

1. Court Poetry: Sidney and Spenser.

Sir Philip Sidney (1554 – 1586) was born of a high aristocratic family, his grandfather being a duke and his uncle an earl and his father a baronet and thrice the lord-deputy of Ireland. He graduated from Oxford and travelled extensively on the Continent of Europe and got acquainted with the humanists in France, Italy and Germany. Besides being a writer he was known as a courtier, a diplomat and a soldier. He was acquainted with many prominent literary figures of the day, including the poet Edmund Spenser, and with him and others he formed a literary circle known as the "Areopagus" and they compared themselves to the well-known group of French humanists and poets the Pléiade (including chiefly Ronsard and Du Bellay). Sidney was married but Penelope Devereux, the woman he loved before his marriage, was the subject of his cycle of 108 love sonnets entitled "Astrophel and Stella". In 1584 he was appointed governor of Flushing, on the coast of the Netherlands, and in 1586, engaged in fighting with Spain he died at the battle of Zutphen in Flanders, at the age of 32.

Sidney is chiefly known and remembered for his three works which established respectively his reputation as poet, romancer and critic: his sonnet sequence "Astrophel and Stella", his prose romance "Arcadia" and his critical essay "The Defence of Poesie" (or "Apology for Poetry").

"Astrophel and Stella" ("Astrophel" being a Greek word meaning "lover of a star" that refers to Sidney himself, while "Stella" being a Latin word that means "star" and refers to Penelope Devereux) was written by Sidney to celebrate his love for Penelope Devereux whom he met and loved in his early days and had the prospect of marrying but who later was married to some one else. Very definitely under the influence of the great Italian humanist poet Petrarch who wrote his cycle of sonnets in honour of Laura , Sidney was the first in England to write a whole series of sonnets (108 in all) plus eleven songs to form a consecutive sequence to celebrate his love for a woman. Some of these songs and sonnets achieved high lyrical excellence and had great influence upon later English poets. This collection, published in 1591, was followed by no less than nine other sonnet sequences by other poets in five years' time, including those by Shakespeare, Spenser ("Amoretti"), Samuel Daniel ("Delia"), Michael Drayton ("Idea") and Thomas Lodge ("Phillis"). Though these sonnets of Sidney's all followed the conventions of Petrarch and frequently showed much artificiality in the elaborate rationalizings about love and in their exuberant and excessively rich and ornamental language, at least some among them did reveal genuine feelings of the poet, and as personal expressions of earthly love they represent the humanist outcry against medieval asceticism. And, amidst the usually involved and weighty expressions, we find among the best poems in the sequence simple yet adroit revelations of the poet's true sentiments, particularly in the famous 1st, 31st and 39th sonnets of the collection (being respectively, "Loving in truth, and fain in verse my love to show", "With how sad steps, 0 moon, thou climb'st the skies!" and "Come, Sleep! 0 Sleep, the certain knot of peace") and also the eleventh of the songs (beginning with " 'Who is it that this dark night"). Especially well-known is the last line in the first sonnet: " 'Fool,' said my Muse to me, 'look in thy heart and write.' "

"Arcadia", a pastoral romance written by Sidney for the amusement of his sister the Countess of Pembroke and published posthumously in 1590, is the earliest specimen of pastoral literature in England and may be traced back to the Italian writer Jacopo Sannazzaro's "Arcadia" (1504) and the Spanish writer Jorge de Montemayor's "Diana Enamorada" (1552) and even to the old pastoral tradition of the ancient Roman poet Vergil and the Hellenistic poet Theocritus. However, Sidney here combined the tradition of the chivalrous romance with the pastoral, for against the pastoral background of Arcadia where "shepherd boys pipe as though they would never be old", there is the story of love and chivalry, of wars and intrigue as well as treachery and high passion, told through a long and complicated plot. The story contains few realistic details and no vivid portraits of characters, but it achieved great success with the reading public in its day and is important historically as the first venture in pastoral tradition in English literature, to be followed by Thomas Lodge's "Rosalynde" and Robert Greene's "Menaphon" and then by Shakespeare's "As You Like It" and "The Winter's Tale".

Sidney's "Defence of Poesie" or "Apology for Poetry" (published posthumously in 1595)was written more or less as an answer to a treatise by a Puritan writer Stephen Gosson, entitled "The School of Abuse", which contained an attack against the theatre and all secular literature and which was dedicated to Sidney. In his essay Sidney disagrees with Gosson by declaring the high mission of poetry, that it is not only to be an imitation of nature and therefore to reflect reality but also has the power to instruct as well as to amuse. This last point has ever been an issue in literary criticism, and "Defence of Poesie" is the earliest critical work in English literary history. However, Sidney agrees with Gosson in giving a rather low estimate of English drama of the time and his reason is not to accuse his contemporary playwrights of immorality but to blame them on their departure from the rules of ancient Greek and Roman drama, which chiefly call for the so-called three unities of time, place and action in dramatic presentation and the separation of the comic elements from the tragic. Sidney earned his place of importance in English literature of his time as the earliest writer of a sonnet sequence and a pastoral romance and a critical essay.

Edmund Spenser (1552 – 1590), born in London of a rather poor merchant tailor's family, went to Cambridge University as a sizar, and was much under the influence of Platonism which then had its sway at the university. He graduated in 1573 and received his M.A. in 1576. At first he was inclined to take orders but in 1578 he became secretary to the Bishop of Rochester, and in 1579 he entered the service of the Earl of Leicester, favourite courtier of Queen Elizabeth. Through Leicester Spenser got acquainted with Philip Sidney and he and Sidney and others formed the literary circle known as the "Areopagus". In 1580 Spenser was appointed secretary to Lord Grey of Wilton, Deputy of Ireland, and from then on to 1598, except for two visits to London of two years each, he remained in Ireland. He received various offices in Ireland under Lord Grey who was carrying out the English governmental policy of tyrannical rule over Ireland, and Spenser obviously shared his views. In 1588 Spenser bought some three thousand acres of land at Kilcolman in County Cork and also the office of Clerk of the Council of Munster. In 1589 he returned to England, now under the protection of Sir Walter Raleigh, and tried to win favour from Queen Elizabeth by dedicating to her what he had written of his epic "The Faerie Queene" but all he obtained seemed to be a pension of 50 pounds a year. In 1594 Spenser married Elizabeth Boyle to whom was addressed his sonnet sequence of "Amoretti". In 1595 he returned to England again, and he wrote "A View of the Present State of Ireland" (in prose) in which he showed the typical attitude of a member of the English ruling class in Ireland and advocated ruthless oppression of the Irish people. In 1597 he returned to Kilcolman with his wife and children and became Sheriff of Cork in September, 1598. In October an Irish rising under the Irish Earl of Desmond against English rule broke out and his castle of Kilcolman was burned to the ground. Spenser fled with his wife and children, first to Cork and then to London. In December of that year he arrived back in London, broken down in health, and he died in January, 1599, in destitution.

Spenser's first important poem is "The Shepherd's Calendar" (1579), a pastoral poem consisting of 12 eclogues, one for each month of the year, and written in different metres. All 12 eclogues, with the exception of the first and the last, are in dialogue form, and Colin Clout the shepherd, a figure borrowed from Skelton, appears everywhere, whether by himself or engaged in a dialogue or being referred to by others. The theme of love is the dominant one, either discussed or touched upon in seven of the eclogues (in the 1st, 3rd, 4th, 6th, 8th, 11th and 12th), among which the 4th is a panegyric of the Queen ("fair Eliza") in the form of a love eclogue. The more significant eclogues are those on the theme of religion: in the 9th the poet centred his attack on the loose living and abuses of the Catholic prelates; in the 5th both the Catholic and the Anglican Churches were satirized; in the 2nd the worldliness of the Anglican clergy was criticized; in the 7th proud and ambitious pastors in general were dispraised while good shepherds were honoured. The 10th eclogue is the only one that deals with the poet's complaint over the neglect of poetry in his age. Here, Spenser objects to poets writing for profit or composing rhymes of ribaldry and considers it the poet's mission to persuade people to do good. However, he adopts the typical attitude of a court poet of his day as he advocates wars and jousts to be proper themes for poetry and calls for panegyrics to "fair Eliza" the queen.

"Amoretti", a sonnet sequence of 88 love poems, and "Epithalamion", a wedding song, were written to celebrate the poet's love and marriage to his wife Elizabeth Boyle. Though the poet was obviously expressing his true sentiments, yet these poems were marred by the influence of Platonism and of religious and mystical concepts of love, so that they sound rather conventional and flat. Similarly, though his "Four Hymns" ("Hymns to Love and Beauty" and "Hymns to Heavenly Love and Heavenly Beauty") may suggest the poet's humanist views on love and beauty as sources of joy, in opposition to the asceticism of the medieval church, yet they betray the strong influence of Neo-Platonism which suggests earthly love and earthly beauty as no more than reflections of heavenly love and heavenly beauty.

"The Faerie Queene" has been regarded by many critics and literary historians as Spenser's masterpiece and as one of the great poems in the English language. The poem is an epic, and according to the author's original plan was to consist of 12 books but only six books and two cantos of the seventh book were completed. According to the poet's letter to Sir Walter Raleigh (prefixed to the 1590 edition of the first three books of the poem), the aim of the epic was "to fashion a gentleman or noble person in virtuous and gentle discipline" and therefore the poet "chose the history of King Arthur" and tried "to portray in Arthur ... the image of a brave knight, perfected in the twelve private moral virtues, as Aristotle hath devised." Thus the 12 books were to give the adventures of twelve knights who stand for twelve different virtues, and the beginning of the story, again according to the letter mentioned above, was to be told in the 12th or the last book where the Faerie Queene (Gloriana, who represents Queen Elizabeth) keeps "her annual feast 12 days" on each of which a separate knight is to be sent forth to seek for adventures. Though only six books and a little more were finished upon the death of the poet, the six knights in their adventures are supposed to represent the six virtues of Holiness, Temperance, Chastity, Friendship, Justice and Courtesy, with the seventh book supposed to suggest the virtue of Constancy. Thus the long epic (each of the six books containing 12 cantos of which each comprises of 30 to 80 nine-line stanzas) is a vivid narrative of knightly adventures with rather involved moral, religious and political allegories, and all sorts of supernatural beings including gods and goddesses, magicians and sorceresses, fairies and giants and monsters, dragons and lions, and serpents and fauns and satyrs, are set against a fantastic background of castles and caves, the House of Mammon, the House of Alma, the Bower of Bliss and other strange and remote places.

Though Spenser's age was a much belated one for medieval chivalry of knightly jousts against monsters and devils to save ladies from distress, and though "The Faerie Queene" was written by the poet both to show his attainments to grand poetic flights in an epic and to curry royal favour by eulogizing "that greatest glorious queen of Faery Lond", yet Spenser as a minor courtier and aristocrat was obviously trying his best to give expression in the *magnum opus* to his ideals of noble knights and virtuous ladies in their struggles against the world's evil forces natural and supernatural.

So "a gentle Knight" and "a lovely Lady" were vividly pictured in colourful language and downright seriousness:

> "A gentle Knight was pricking on the plaine,
> Ycladd in mightie armes and silver shielde,
> Wherein old dints of deepe woundes did remaine,
> The cruell markes of many a bloody fielde;
> Yet armes till that time did he never wield.
> His angry steede did chide his foming bitt,
> As much disdayning to the curbe to yield:
> Full jolly knight he seemd, and faire did sitt,
> As one for knightly giusts and fierce encounters fitt."
>
> (Book I, Canto I, Stanza 1)

and

> "A lovely Ladie rode him faire beside,
> Upon a lowly Asse more white then snow,
> Yet she much whiter; but the same did hide
> Under a vele, that whimpled was full low;
> And over all a blacke stole shee did thraw:
> As one that inly mournd, so was she sad,
> And heavie sate upon her palfrey slow;
> Seemed in heart some hidden care she had,

　　　　And by her, in a line, a milkewhite lambe she lad."

(Book I, Canto I, Stanza 4)

The ideas here may be stilted and archaic, but they are vested in picturesque words and leisurely phrasing, and the beauty of poetic form has been a great attraction to later poets and readers through the centuries.

However, though many of the persons and scenes in the poem may be rather vividly described and the purpose of the poet was certainly to praise the virtuous and censure the wicked, yet the abstract ideas presented by the intricate and obscure allegorical imageries point unmistakably to the essentially aristocratic nature of the epic. Though there may be found certain traces of the humanist philosophy of the Renaissance, such as the adventurous spirit of the age, the joy of present life, the love of nature and natural beauty and the eulogy of the power and capabilities of man, these are placed in the curious environment of medieval chivalry and Puritan ethics, while the praise of abstract moral virtues and the denunciation of mystical evils are only part of the mental outlook of an aristocratic gentleman at the court of Queen Elizabeth. Nevertheless, the poetry was written with great technical skill both from the point of view of its music and metre and from that of rich imageries and ornate language, and it is chiefly this achievement in poetic beauty that earned for Spenser the distinction of "the poets' poet" and led to the great influence of the poem upon a number of great English poets in the later centuries, including especially the 19th-century poets Byron, Shelley, Keats and Tennyson. And the Spenserian Stanza (a 9-line stanzaic form used in this epic with the rhyme scheme of ababbcbcc and with the first eight lines in iambic pentametre and the last or 9th line an alexandrine) became a popular verse form in the historical development of English poetry.

"The Faerie Queene" was truly a poetic feat in its day, though it is now generally admired only for its memorable poetic imageries and its enchanting metre and rhythm, and for the aristocratic ideals of a bygone age.

2. Prose Fiction: Lyly, Lodge, Greene, Sidney, Nashe, Deloney.

In the last decades of the 16th century both romances and realistic fiction flourished in England, including John Lyly's euphuistic prose, the romances of Lodge and Greene and Sidney and the fictional works of Nashe and Deloney.

John Lyly (1553 – 1606) was the oldest of the so-called "University Wits" most of whom distinguished themselves as dramatists, but Lyly was first of all a writer of prose fiction and only secondarily a playwright. He was born of a scholar's family. His grandfather William Lily was a Greek grammarian, a humanist and a friend of Thomas More and Erasmus. Lyly himself went to Oxford University and thence to London, where he lived as a writer under the patronage of Lord Burley. In 1578, at the age of 24, he published "Euphues, or the Anatomy of Wit", which won immediate acclaim, and in 1580 came the sequel, "Euphues and His England". The success of these two prose works led him to the writing of court plays. A total of eight comedies in prose, with inserted lyrics, were written by Lyly from 1584 to 1601, and presented not by professional actors at the regular theatres of the time but by children's companies at the court of Queen Elizabeth.

In"Euphues, or the Anatomy of Wit"the hero Euphues or the Well-Endowed is a young Athenian (i.e., an Oxford man), noble, handsome, quick-witted and with a passion for travelling, but too little disciplined by education. He goes to Naples (i.e., London) and is deaf to the advice of a wise old man who warns him of the vices of the town. He enjoys himself very much there, frequenting parties and festivities and falling in love with his good friend Philautus' lady-love Lucilla. Euphues succeeds in winning her love and quarrels with Philautus and is about to marry her when she gives him up in favour of a third and unworthy suitor. Euphues then leaves Naples in disgust and returns to Athens, the city of philosophers, to spend his time among his books. The story is a thin one, and is broken up by much irrelevant material, including a treatise on education which contains sharp criticism of the conditions at Oxford. The book was extremely popular, reaching 4 editions in 18 months.

"Euphues and His England" is in theme very different from, in fact quite the opposite to, the earlier volume. Here, in the place of a strong satire on women in the first book, is to be found the author's eulogy of his country, its queen, its universities, and above all, its ladies. ("There is no beautie but in England". The heroines are models of constancy and virtue, and peace and religion reign under Elizabeth.) Here, Euphues and Philautus are co-heroes and they come to England and spend some time at the court. Philautus makes love to a court beauty, Lady Camilla, who rejects him, and he then, with the help of an elderly woman Lady Flavia, forms a platonic friendship with the latter's niece Frances. Euphues, on the other hand, after another quarrel with Philautus, withdraws himself first to study, and then to a mountain. The book also contains witty and realistic scenes of the London society.

The important thing about the two books lies not so much in the stories therein as in the style of the language used, though the stories themselves, while showing Italian influence, did contain some mild social satire with sketchy pictures of the idle life at the court and in the universities, and in this sense they were significant departures from the tradition of fantastic medieval romances and pointed toward an initial interest in the depicting of contemporary life. However, it is the euphuistic style, with the employment of extremely artificial language, that chiefly attracted public attention at the time. On the whole euphuism is comparable to the verse-like prose of the Six Dynasties in our Chinese literary history. The first peculiarity of the style is the use of balanced sentence construction, and other artificial elaborations in language, including antithesis and alliteration. Sometimes alliterations are doubled up, either direct or crossed (e.g., "The hot liver of a heedless lover", or "Let my rude birth excuse my bold request", or "Although I have shrined thee in my heart for a trusty friend, I will shun thee hereafter as a trothless foe"). The second peculiarity is the employment of images and similes taken either from ancient mythology and history or from classical and medieval "unnatural" natural history, and also the use of quotations from and references to classical authors. These peculiarities resulted inevitably in extremely affected and unnatural language, overburdened with rich ornaments and elaborate decorations.

For a time after the publication of these two works, Euphuism became the fashion in English literature and many prose writers, including Robert Greene and Thomas Lodge and even the young Shakespeare, began to imitate the rich and artificial euphuistic language, though there were other writers, like Philip Sidney and Nashe and Deloney, who were opposed to Lyly's style and wrote very differently.

Alongside of Lyly's two books on Euphues, a number of prose romances, some of them of pastoral tradition, also catered to the aristocratic tastes of the age. Sidney's "Arcadia" was followed by Lodge's "Rosalynde" and Greene's "Menaphon" and "Pandosto", though "Rosalynde" was also partly under the influence of Euphuism. These romances were rather flat, conventional and artificial works and had little importance except for their influence upon some of Shakespeare's plays.

More important are the realistic works of prose fiction in late 16th-century England. These were related in a way to many autobiographical pamphlets written by a number of writers at the time, pamphlets which in dealing with the authors' autobiographical reminiscences touched upon pictures of social life in London and other locales. Especially well-known were such pamphlets by Robert Greene who in writing about his own experiences in life gave vivid representations of the underworld of London, particularly about the rogues and the tricks they played, and this led to the so-called "picaresque" stories which were essentially plebeian in nature and written for the plebeian readers and among which Nashe's "The Unfortunate Traveller" has often been considered the earliest specimen of importance.

Thomas Nashe (1567 – 1601), son of a clergyman and a sizar at Cambridge University, was the youngest of the so-called "University Wits". He was a pamphleteer of social satires and also the author of two plays, but has been chiefly known as the author of "The Unfortunate Traveller, or the Life of Jack Wilton" (1594).

The story is supposed to be based on historical facts, dealing with the life of Jack Wilton, a page in the reign of Henry VIII and later an unscrupulous adventurer who wandered through Flanders, Germany and Italy, met many famous people and witnessed many famous scenes. Actually here we find a strange mixture of historical, semi-historical as well as purely imaginary events arranged in a haphazard fashion, without any consideration for chronological order. Wilton started out by playing knavish tricks during his participation in the siege of Tourney and then he ran away from the camp. He was present at Münster in Germany and witnessed the conflict between the German Emperor and the Anabaptists and the subsequent hanging of John of Leyden. He then entered into the service of the Earl of Surrey and travelled with the poet through many different countries on the European continent. Passing through Rotterdam he met Erasmus and Thomas More and watched the former writing his "Praise of Folly" and the latter meditating over his "Utopia". Then at Wittenburg in Germany he saw an academic pageant and an old play and also religious disputes between Martin Luther and Carolostadius, and then got acquainted with the famous magician Cornelius Agrippa. Then at Venice he passed himself off as the Earl of Surrey and ran away with the courtesan of an Italian nobleman, and then he was overtaken by the Earl of Surrey who forgave him and he witnessed Surrey defeating all comers at a tournament in Florence in honour of his lady-love Geraldine. Wilton then left Surrey's service and went to Rome just at the time of the outbreak of the plague, and realistic pictures were given of scenes of violence and tragedy there, including rapes and robberies and murders as well as tortures and executions. The narrative ends with the repentance of Wilton, his marriage to the Italian courtesan and his return to the English king's camp.

"The Unfortunate Traveller", as the first important picaresque novel in the English language, fell definitely under the influence of the Spanish rogue stories or picaresque tales ("picaro" in Spanish meaning "rogue") which were of wide popularity in 16th-century England.

The language used here is more natural and stands in direct opposition to the artificiality of euphuism.

Of Thomas Deloney (1543 – 1600) little is known. At one time he worked as a silk weaver in Norwich. Later he must have moved to London (probably by 1586); before 1596 he must have written some fifty ballads and broadsides, but in 1596 he incurred official anger for having introduced the queen into one of his ballads in "fond and indecent sort", and was forced, in consequence, to seek temporary hiding. From then on, he turned to the writing of prose narratives, and between 1596 and 1600 he produced three such narratives: "Thomas of Reading", "Jack of Newbury" and "The Gentle Craft". He died in extreme poverty.

Half a century ago Deloney was known as merely a writer of ballads, and only at the beginning of the 20th century was he discovered as the author of the three works of prose fiction. Though his ballads were popular at the time, Deloney's chief contribution to English literature lies in the field of prose fiction.

Each of Deloney's three tales deals with a trade: "Jack of Newbury" about the weavers, "The Gentle Craft" about the shoemakers, and "Thomas of Reading" about the clothiers. Though in each novel Deloney describes the apprentices as well as the masters of the trade concerned, more attention is paid to the masters and their families and their relations with the nobility or the king, or at least to the apprentices or journeymen who later rise to the position of masters through marriage or other means. So in these narratives the pictures given are chiefly those of the upper layers of the city plebeians, and poor artisans or handicraftsmen are only occasionally and rather briefly described.

"Jack of Newbury" tells chiefly about a weaver named John Winchcomb (a historical figure of a wealthy Berkshire weaver, 1470 – 1514), an apprentice who was wooed and won by his master's widow and thereby attained to affluent circumstances, and who later entertained Henry VIII in his Newbury home, spoke frankly in the king's presence and helped his fellow weavers in Cardinal Wolsey's despite. While there are comic episodes and digressions interspersed here and there in the course of the narrative, with a streak of the light and the ludicrous running through even the serious accounts of courtship between the master's widow and the apprentice and of the official meeting and conversation between the king and the master weaver, the most significant social reality represented in this work of prose fiction was the growing voice and power of the rising bourgeoisie (i.e., the master weavers including John Winchcomb and his friends, who not only could help the king and the court but also were capable of resisting unreasonable royal prerogatives that ran counter to their bourgeois interests). This is most clearly shown in the master weaver Winchcomb's rather insolent speeches addressed to the king, when the leader of "the work-loving ants" (as Winchcomb thus refers to himself and to his weavers) speaks most straightforwardly of his wish to defend his friends and workers from any encroachments of their interests by the idle and power-loving butterflies (meaning the aristocracy). Also, in Winchcomb's actions to assist his fellow weavers in defiance of unjust orders from Cardinal Wolsey may be seen once again the bourgeoisie's strength and its readiness to struggle against the authority of the king and the court if its own interests were challenged or endangered. In this sense this novel may be said to reflect rather directly the sentiments of the parliamentary forces that represented chiefly the interests of the bourgeoisie but pretended to stand also for those of the workers or artisans, in their struggles with the monarch and the aristocracy, in the last decades of the 16th century.

At the same time, "Jack of Newbury" contains some vivid descriptions of the weavers at work as well as the songs supposed to be sung while they worked. Here we may see the gradual development of handicraft workshops into fair-sized factories in 16th-century England, for in Winchcomb's big weaver's shop there were no less than 200 looms, each worked by one man with a boy to help him, 100 women carders and 200 spinners, 150 children who pick the wool, 50 shearers, 80 rovers and 20 fullers. Though a rosy picture is given here of the general contentment and joy of the weavers at work, of the beautiful clothes worn by these artisans and of their joyful songs accompanying their work, and though we are told how Winchcomb upbraids his wife for giving his apprentices short rations and insisting on providing them with ample food, yet in the book here and there appear also bits of descriptions of the great misery of half-starved wool-picking children and shearers, that at least reveals the author's sympathy for the oppressed and exploited masses of workers in his day.

"Thomas of Reading" deals chiefly with the incidents in the lives of six master clothiers supposed to belong to the reign of Henry I (in the first half of the 12th century), but actually the details must have been drawn from the author's own time. Here, as in "Jack of Newbury", the writer tells of the great wealth of these master clothiers and of the intimate relations between these prominent citizens of the kingdom and the king. The king, while travelling on the road and meeting with the long lines of waggons that carry the manufactured cloth, has to step aside to let the traffic pass, and later he entertains them and acknowledges their contributions to the nation's wealth and their important position in society. In this novelette, there are also some light and humorous and even comic episodes at the inns and among the gossiping wives of the clothiers, aside from a somewhat tragic love story about Duke Robert, the king's brother. Artistically this narrative suffers from a lack of unity, Thomas of Reading being only one of the clothiers from the West Country who figure as the chief characters in the story.

"The Gentle Craft" consists of a series of tales giving a survey of shoemakers from the legendary times. The first two of these tales, about St. Hugh the patron saint of the gentle craft of shoemaking who became a martyr at the time of the Roman Emperor Diocletian, and about the brothers Crispin and Crispinian who suffered from persecution under the Roman Emperor Maximillian but who later triumphed, were written in the romantic and euphuistic tradition. The third and most important tale in the series is about Simon Eyre (at the time of Henry VI in the 15th century) who rose from a shoemaker's apprentice to the position of lord mayor, founded the leather-market in Leadenhall and started a holiday on which shoemakers' apprentices were given free feasts at his cost. This part of the book inspired the play "The Shoemaker's Holiday" (acted in 1599) by the plebeian dramatist Thomas Dekker. The next story is about Richard Castelar of the time of Henry VIII who while yet an apprentice was involved in a strange love intrigue with Long Meg of Westminster, a colourful semi-historical and semi-legendary figure of a serving-maid and then a public-house keeper in London, but who later became rich and upon his death bequeathed his fortune to the poor and to the hospitals. The next story is about a master shoemaker Master Peachey giving some court bullies heavy beatings and about Peachey's journeyman Tom Drum experiencing rebuff in love-making from a widow. The last story in the series is concerned with the shoemaker Anthony Now-Now who mixes with tavern-haunters and minstrels. "The Gentle Craft" contains some light and humorous passages and occasional comic scenes, as well as realistic pictures of apprentices and journeymen at work and of maid-servants in the taverns and other ordinary London citizens of the day.

Deloney's three works of prose fiction started a new tradition of narratives about the city people connected with different handicraft trades. He spoke chiefly for the masters of the trades or at least apprentices-turned-masters, in other words, for the rising bourgeoisie, but because the line dividing the masters and the apprentices was not so clear-cut at the time, he also spoke partly on behalf of the apprentices and the lower strata of the city plebeians of the day or at least had much sympathy for those hardworking artisans. The language used occasionally shows the unhealthy influence of euphuism, but on the whole, when the author wrote about realistic incidents in the lives of the weavers or shoemakers, whether masters or journeymen or apprentices, and their wives and the serving-maids and the common people they associated with, he generally employed simple and natural lauguage that represented the real speech of the people.

Deloney's books were popular during his lifetime and after. "Jack of Newbury" is known to have reached its eleventh edition by the year

1630, and was re-issued in the 18th century. But after that these fictional works were forgotten and had to be re-discovered at the beginning of the present century.

3. **Pre-Shakespearean Drama: English Drama under Classical Influence; The University Wits: Lyly, Peele, Lodge, Nashe, Greene, Kyd and Marlowe.**

As David Lyndsay and John Heywood held the stage in early 16th-century England, the revival of learning which began in the last years of the 15th century and became the rage in the early 16th brought along with it the classical drama of ancient Greece and Rome, particularly of the latter. This classical influence upon English drama developed in three marked stages: first the acting of classical dramas of Roman writers in the original, in Latin, in schools and especially in the universities; then the translation into English of the tragedies of Seneca and the comedies of Plautus and Terence and the staging of these dramas in translation; and finally the writing and the production of plays in English, more or less in imitation of these ancient Roman dramas or at least in strict adherence to the dramatic rules or laws formulated upon the typical specimens of classical drama. The first two stages took place chiefly in the early decades of the 16th century, and the third and last stage in the 1550's and 1560's.

In the two middle decades the earliest regular comedies and tragedies in the English language were written, and in them the elements of church drama, especially of the moralities and interludes of the early 16th century, plus those of the different types of folk drama, were merged with those of the classical drama, and these invigorated new dramas paved the way for the flowering of dramatic art in England in the last two decades of the 16th century, with the production of the plays of the University Wits and of the early Shakespeare.

The first regular English comedy, "Ralph Roister Doister", was written around 1550 (acted in the early 1550's and printed in about 1567) by Nicholas Udall (1505 – 1556), who was headmaster successively of Eton and Westminster and made translations of Terence's plays. Written in verse, this comedy followed the tradition of the plays of Plautus and Terence both in dramatic structure and in character portrayal, as the author openly avowed in the Prologue. The titular hero, Ralph Roister Doister, a swaggering simpleton of a soldier, tries to woo a wealthy and handsome widow, Christian Custance, and his friend the mischievous Matthew Merrygreek urges him on, but the widow who is betrothed to a London merchant Gawin Goodluck repulses Ralph and with the aid of her servants beats him and drives him out, and eventually Goodluck is reconciled to the widow after having been deceived at first by false reports. In this play of five acts, more or less modelled after Plautus, there are however traces of the morality plays to be found in the personified names of Goodluck the merchant and Constance (Custance) the widow and in the resemblance of the character of Merrygreek to the type figure of Vice. But the most important thing about this comedy is the realistic representation here of the social life of the London plebeians, narrated with much fun and humour, and it is highly significant and indicative of the rise of the bourgeoisie in England at the time that the merchant finally triumphs over the swaggering Ralph who is a gentleman.

Another early comedy, sometimes known as the second regular English comedy in verse, is "Gammer Gurton's Needle" (acted in the 1560's and printed in 1575), of which the authorship is uncertain (William Stevenson or John Still, in either case Fellow of Cambridge University). This comedy is more definitely English, with a true native English theme though absorbing the elements both of the English church drama and of classical drama. Gammer (Grandma) Gurton loses the needle with which she has sewed breeches for her servant Hodge and fails to find it anywhere. The good-for-nothing Diccon (resembling Vice in the moralities) persuades the Gammer that her friend Dame Chat of the alehouse has stolen it. This leads to much quarrel and heavy beatings between the two women and the curate Dr. Rat also gets involved and has his head broken. Finally the matter is brought to the court and there as Diccon slaps Hodge on the buttock, the latter feels acute pain and then draws out the needle which has been hidden in his breeches all that time. The story, set in "a village in England", is simple and does not have any depth of meaning, but it is vividly told in a series of lively and realistic scenes of great fun and laughter which reflect to a certain extent the social life in the English countryside of the time.

In the field of tragedy, the earliest regular English tragedy is "Gorboduc, or Ferrex and Porrex" (acted first in 1561), written jointly by Thomas Norton (1532 – 1584) and Thomas Sackville (1536 – 1608), the first three acts by the former and the last two by the latter. The play is constructed on the model of a Senecan tragedy and the subject is taken from the legendary chronicles of Britain according to Geoffrey of Monmouth. Gorboduc and Videna are king and queen and Gorboduc divides his kingdom between his two sons Ferrex and Porrex and a quarrel arises between the two. Porrex kills Ferrex and is killed in revenge by their mother Videna, and then the people rise and kill both Gorboduc and Videna, and finally a civil war ensues as the feudal lords fight for the throne. Strict observance of the classical rules of tragedy is made here, including the five-act division, the so-called dramatic unities of time, place and action, the exclusion of all comic elements from tragedy, the absence of stage action, the narration of action in the speeches, the use of the chorus and of messengers and parasites, etc. The play was not effective dramatically, but it had a most significant theme for the age when all England after having suffered much from feudal wars in the 15th century was worried now in the 16th over the problem of succession to the throne, with Queen Elizabeth unmarried and without a definite successor. The importance of political unity and the abhorrence of civil wars were clearly voiced in this play. Also, "Gorboduc" was the first English tragedy written in blank verse and in this way anticipated the numerous great tragedies in the late 16th century in England written in the same verse form.

After the 1550's and the 1560's, quite a number of plays were written and staged but unfortunately most of these were later lost. A new type, the chronicle history play which drew its material from early English history, appeared, anticipating similar plays by Shakespeare and his immediate predecessors the University Wits.

The professional performances of regular English comedies and tragedies were at first given at the inn yards, or at the inns of court or private residences of noblemen or at the royal court, but gradually greater demand for more space for actors and for the audience led to the construction of regular theatres. The first of such regular threatres for public performances was built in London in 1576, and then theatrical activities prospered so much in the Elizabethan age that by 1600 there were already 11 theatres in and about London, among which were the Globe and the Blackfriars where Shakespeare's plays were performed. Theatres were of two kinds, private and public. The private theatres were more richly built and decorated, completely roofed, lighted by candles, and furnished with painted scenes, and were chiefy performed before royal and noble audiences who paid higher admission charges. The public theatres were three stories high, were round, octagonal, or square in shape, had a pit or central portion open to the sky and without seats, and were surrounded by balconies with cushioned seats. The front stage jutted out into the pit and at first there was no scenery, as in the old Chinese theatres for Peking opera. Gradually there were professional companies of actors, besides child actors. There were no actresses, women's parts being played by boys.

The immediate predecessors of Shakespeare were a group of men from the two universities of Oxford and Cambridge, who were generally known as the University Wits, including John Lyly, George Peele (1558 – 1598), Thomas Lodge (1558 – 1625), Robert Greene (1558–1592), Thomas Nashe, Thomas Kyd (1558 – 1594), and Christopher Marlowe (1564 – 1593), Lyly and Peele and Lodge being from Oxford and Greene and Nashe and Marlowe from Cambridge while Kyd also likely to have received a university education. Of these seven writers, Lodge is chiefly remembered for his pastoral romance "Rosalynde" and hardly known as a playwright, having written only one insignificant play, while Nashe, with two unimportant dramas to his credit, is also known almost solely for his picaresque romance "The Unfortunate Traveller, or the Life of Jack Wilton". Peele wrote several dramas, but they were known primarily for the lyrics in them.

"The Old Wives' Tale", his best known play, contains a fantastic and romantic story not unlike that in Milton's masque "Comus", but here the tale of two brothers and their sister getting lost in the woods at night and of the three fallen into the power of an evil conjurer and finally rescued by Eumenides the wandering knight, is filled with the supernatural and the impossible and lacks the moral idealism in Milton's drama. Lyly's fame rests chiefly on his two works on Euphues, and his plays are only significant as the earliest dramatic works of the University Wits, the first romantic comedies (also the first pastoral dramas) and the earliest specimens of the blending of the poetic or the lyrical with the prosaic in drama. Containing witty dialogue and pretty lyrics and artistic finish in plot construction Lyly's plays were nevertheless court dramas written for the aristocratic few and in this sense fell far behind the more popular dramas of Shakespeare and Marlowe and even of Kyd.

Thomas Kyd (1558–1594) is important chiefly for his revenge play, "The Spanish Tragedy" which was produced about 1585, went through at least 10 printed editions before 1634 and continued to hold the stage until the closing of the theatres in 1642. The son of a scrivener, Kyd was educated at the Merchant Taylors' School in London and probably followed his father's profession for a time, but there is no evidence of his ever entering a university. He was a friend of Christopher Marlowe's with whom he shared lodgings in about 1591. In 1593 he was arrested and tortured, under the suspicion of treasonable activity, and in his room were found certain "atheistic" disputations denying the deity of Jesus Christ. He probably died in debt in 1594.

Kyd followed the tradition of the Roman dramatist Seneca and adopted in "The Spanish Tragedy" the theme of revenge, the murder of a relative, the appearance of ghosts, the element of lunacy and a play within a play. He employed much declamation and soliloquy in rhetorical verse. He also made use of the native English dramatic forms inherited from the miracle and morality plays of the Middle Ages. His outstanding contribution to the historical development of English drama consists in the influence of "The Spanish Tragedy" and its hero

Hieronimo upon Shakespeare's play "Hamlet". In fact, Kyd may also have written an earlier version of "Hamlet", known to scholars as "Ur-Hamlet". "The Spanish Tragedy" is also known for the use of blank verse, rhymed couplets and prose to adapt to different moods and occasions in the drama.

Robert Greene represented the adventurous spirit and the resourcefulness and many-sidedness of the man of the Renaissance in England. Educated at Cambridge and widely travelled in Italy and Spain, Greene spent the important decade of his brief life in London, leading a Bohemian existence among the writers and actors and the plebeians of the English capital and writing rather voluminously all sorts of things, from lyrical poems and dramas and prose romances to pamphlets and autobiographical reminiscences and confessions. While several of his prose romances and personal confessions were well known in their day and some of his lyrics attained to certain heights in poetic beauty, his significance lies chiefly in his dramas.

Among Greene's memorable plays should be mentioned "Friar Bacon and Friar Bungay" (1589), "The Scottish History of King James the Fourth" (1591) and, probably also of his authorship, "A Pleasant Conceited Comedy of George a Greene, the Pinner of Wakefield" (1588?). "Friar Bacon and Friar Bungay" deals with a story about magic not unsimilar to Marlowe's "Doctor Faustus" and reflects the desire of the men of the Renaissance to probe into the secrets of nature even by means of magic. Friar Bacon and Friar Bungay are historical figures represented as magicians who try to make the devil speak. The play also tells the romantic love story of the daughter of the keeper of Fressingfield who is loved both by the Prince of Wales and by Lord Lacy and who is finally won by Lacy when the prince yields in his favour. The picture of Margaret in her dairy, though she is actually the keeper's daughter and not a peasant girl, gives us nevertheless a very fresh portrait of a simple and charming country maiden against an attractive background of the countryside.

In "James IV" Greene censured Machiavellianism in the Scottish king's courtier Ateukin and showed his obvious disapproval of the lascivious king while he idealized Dorothea the virtuous queen. Dorothea's disguise as a man, a dramatic device used for the first time by Greene, was later brought to perfection by Shakespeare in his several comedies, "The Two Gentlemen of Verona," "The Merchant of Venice", "As You Like It", "Twelfth Night" and "Cymbeline".

More noteworthy is "The Pinner of Wakefield". Here the hero is a yeoman, George a Greene, the pinner of Wakefield, and here also appear Robin Hood and Maid Marian and his followers Scarlet and Much. The pinner, loyal to the English king, captures traitors and sends them to the monarch but when King Edward wants to make him a knight, he declines the honour and expresses his wish to remain a yeoman. On the other hand, he thinks much of Robin Hood and his men and welcomes them to his home after having unknowingly fought with them. Bettris, daughter of a landlord, loves the poor pinner in spite of her father's objections. The play is loosely constructed around the hero, but in the pinner we see a figure who comes truly from the common people, and this was a very unusual practice in dramas of that age. Besides, in spite of his loyalty toward the king, he is not ashamed of his poverty and low station in life but does things freely in accordence with what he considers to be right. Also, in this play, Jane a Barley who defies oppression is praised, while the oppressor King James of Scotland is punished. However, Robin Hood and his men are not well portrayed here, and the clowning of Jenkin, our hero's servant, and of the shoemakers is rather pointless. Taken as a whole, the play with a yeoman as the hero and with scenes set in the countryside, is something fresh and new in Elizabethan drama and must have exerted its wholesome influence upon Shakespeare's comedies with similar backgrounds, such as "As You Like It" and "The Winter's Tale".

The most prominent figure among the University Wits is Christopher Marlowe (1564 – 1593). Born in the same year as Shakespeare, he was the son of a shoemaker at Canterbury. He was educated at Cambridge University (1581 – 87) and then he went to London and lived and wrote there until he died (1587 – 93). The traditional story about Marlowe's untimely death, that he was stabbed at a tavern brawl, whether over love or money, has since been largely discredited by recent research. Though not everything has been cleared up, his death was quite possibly the result of murder or assassination by the secret police of the time, under the directions of the Privy Council. It has been suggested that Marlowe belonged to one of the more radical literary circles, Sir Walter Raleigh's group, that he was an active atheist who preached irreligion if not also composed irreligious tracts and was therefore ever under the watchful eyes of the Privy Council and its secret agents, that he was arrested at least on two occasions on one of which he had to endure a fortnight's imprisonment, and that his death was due to political reasons, probably as a result of attacks from two government spies. But whatever his personal career, Marlowe was a great poet and dramatist, who wrote in the brief space of six or seven years seven dramas, a long narrative poem "Hero and Leander" (left unfinished upon his death and later completed by a fellow poet and dramatist George Chapman), and some short lyrics including "The Passionate Shepherd to His Love" (or "Come live with me, and be my love"). Of the seven dramas two are less important: "The Massacre at Paris" which was left unfinished and which was about the massacre of St. Bartholomew and the egoistic ambition of the Duke of Guise; and "The Tragedy of Dido" which was a dramatization of the fourth book of Vergil's "The Aeneid" and was finished by Nashe. The other five are, in the probable chronological order of their writing: "Tamburlaine the Great", Parts I and II (1587 – 1588); "The Tragical History of Doctor Faustus" (1589?); "The Jew of Malta" (1590?) and "Edward the Second" (1592 – 93).

"Tamburlaine the Great" contains two parts and ten acts, being two plays with a continuous story, that of the rise and fall of the hero Tamburlaine, or Timur, the Tartar king whose biographies by a Spanish writer Pedro Maxia and by an Italian named Perondinus had inspired Marlowe. Part I tells of the steady rise in the career of the Scythian shepherd Tamburlaine until he became the King of Persia and the conqueror of many kings and the Emperor of Turkey as well as the winner of the affection of Zenocrate, the daughter of the Soldan (Sultan) of Egypt. Part II continues with further conquests for Tamburlaine, including victories over kings and princes both Christian and Mohammedan, and then relates the death first of Zenocrate and finally of Tamburlaine himself. Here, while in dramatic form Marlowe followed the medieval concept of tragedy as beginning with the rise of the hero from his humble origin to the zenith of his success and ending with his downfall or death, in theme the poet voiced the supreme desire of the man of the Renaissance for infinite power and authority via the central character Tamburlaine and started the dramatic tradition of "one-man tragedy". Tamburlaine is described as a great though primitive hero who expressed his high ambitions with great eloquence and conquered others with sheer force but who was extremely cruel and brutal toward his enemies while lavish in his love-making. The plot gets a bit monotonous as the cental figure conquers one enemy after another, but the hero's grandiloquent speeches are vested in powerful language and great poetry as Marlowe makes skilful use of blank verse as his medium for tragedy. The two plays were written and staged immediately before and after the great historical event of the defeat of the Spanish Armada, and the military glories of Tamburlaine became a very timely theme to the English audience celebrating their national greatness with strong patriotic feelings.

"The Tragical History of Doctor Faustus" is based on a popular old German legend, but Marlowe reshaped the story freely to suit his own purposes and the play served to express the Renaissance man's desire for infinite power through knowledge. The great scholar Doctor Faustus is not satisfied with the knowledge he already has, and he tries to experiment with magic and calls up Mephistopheles, the Devil's servant, and asks the latter to carry out his errands for him. Mephistopheles makes him sign a compact with the Devil (Lucifer) to surrender his soul to the latter in return for 24 years of life in which he may have the services of Mephistopheles to give him everything he desires. A series of scenes follow, in which with Mephistopheles' aid Faustus is granted all his desires (for a woman, for knowledge about heaven and earth, for the sight of the Pope and the Emperor and of Alexander the

Great, for grapes in the winter season, for a visit from Helen of Troy. etc.) and in which Faustus goes through much mental conflict, symbolized in the appearances of both Good Angel and Evil Angel. Finally the hour comes at the end of the 24 years and Faustus is forced to surrender his soul to the Devil. While this fantastic drama is diverted by many realistic details, Faustus dominates the play throughout and therefore is the hero again of a "one-man tragedy". Though the eventual tragic outcome of the hero seems to suggest the author's disapproval of Faustus' compact with Lucifer, yet the powerful personality of Faustus, his eloquent speeches and particularly his fervent desire for infinite knowledge, depicted so effectively in the play, may point to Marlowe's great sympathy for the hero, especially if we take into account the poet's atheistic attitude or at least his skepticism toward the Christian religion. As in "Tamburlaine the Great", so in "Doctor Faustus" some of the most powerful utterances of the hero are great poetry expressed in forceful and beautiful blank verse which has been called "Marlowe's mighty line" by many critics and literary historians.

"The Jew of Malta" is another expression of the spirit of the Renaissance, the desire for infinite wealth, as it is also a satire on money-worship and Machiavellianism of the age of rising capitalism. The hero of the play, the rich "Jew of Malta", Barabas, is a worshipper and owner of infinite wealth as well as a representative of Machiavellianism. As the play opens, he is shown sitting in his counting house with heaps of gold before him and intoxicated by the immensity of his wealth and the immense power that comes with such wealth. The Grand Seignier of Turkey demands a huge amount of tribute money from the island of Malta and the Maltese governor rules that all the Jews of the island should be deprived of half their property in order to pay the tribute. Barabas resists and is punished by having all his possessions taken from him. By trickery he succeeds in making his daughter Abigail throw bags of money and jewels to him at night, and then to show his hatred for the Christians he writes a false challenge and makes the two Christian suitors of his daughter (including the governor's son) kill each other and then he punishes the daughter for loving one of the Christians by poisoning her. Then, lest his guilt be made known, he, with the help of his Machiavellian slave Ithamore, kills two friars. Ithamore extorts money from Barabas by threatening to betray him but both of them are eventually betrayed by Ithamore's courtesan and her companion, and Barabas barely escapes death by pretending to be dead. He then betrays Malta to the Turks who are besieging the fortress on the island, and he is made governor of Malta by the Turks, but he distrusts the latter and tries to betray them again by inviting the Turkish commander to a banquet where the Turks are to be thrown into a caldron through a collapsible floor. But the Maltese Christians whom Barabas has asked to assist him in the trick to be played upon the Turks betray the Jew, and at the end of the play Barabas himself falls through the collapsible floor into the caldron and dies. Barabas' slave Ithamore is also shown to be a Machiavellian who carries out all the murdering and poisoning for his master and then betrays him, and the author's intention of satirizing Machiavellianism of his day is clearly expressed in the introduction of a character named Machiavel as prologue-speaker. Thus the satire on greed and on the evil deeds that naturally come with greed constitutes the central theme of the play, and Marlowe's humanist ideals led him to criticize the desire for infinite wealth in the primitive accumulation stage of capitalism. "The Jew of Malta" also significantly anticipated Shakespeare's "The Merchant of Venice".

"Edward the Second" tells of the career of Edward II from his accession to his death, including the king's infatuation for his favourite Gaveston, his barons' revolt against him as the result, the capture and death of Gaveston at the hands of the barons, then his infatuation for another favourite Spencer and his estrangement from his queen Isabella, her rebellion with the support of her lover Mortimer, his defeat at a battle and his forced abdication in favour of his son Edward III, and finally his murder and his son Edward III's punishment of Mortimer and Isabella in revenge. There can be no doubt that Marlowe in writing a play like this had in view the numerous favourites at the court of Queen Elizabeth and that the tragedy was apparently written on the one hand against favouritism and absolutism of the monarch and on the other against any possible attempt to restore the feudal barons to power. In plot construction and in character portrayal as well as in the description of the relations between the monarch and the barons, "Edward II" anticipated the history plays of Shakespeare. Even in the blank verse used here there is resemblance to that in some of Shakespeare's history plays, particularly in "Richard II". No wonder Marlowe has frequently been suggested as possibly the collaborator or at least one of the collaborators of Shakespeare's in the latter's earliest history plays like the three parts of "Henry VI".

Marlowe wrote few non-dramatic poems, but his share in "Hero and Leander" (the first two of the six sestiads that make up the poem) shows his power in narrative poetry with a lyrical theme, while his "Come live with me and be my love" is certainly one of the best love lyrics in the Elizabethan age.

But Marlowe was first of all a dramatist, and he was the greatest of the English dramatists before Shakespeare because he represented fully the spirit of the Renaissance and expressed it with such skill in the artistic medium of drama in blank verse. He not only expressed the humanist ideals about the infinite capabilities of man, in the desire for power and knowledge and wealth, which came with the age of primitive accumulation of capital, but he apparently succeeded in seeing the defects beyond the glories of such desire for power and knowledge and wealth and proceeded admirably to satirize such desire and its tragic effects. And in "Edward II" he also voiced the wish of the English people and the English bourgeoisie for political unity under the monarch and censured favouritism at the royal court during the reign of Queen Elizabeth. And always Marlowe showed his great power in creating vivid characters and his superb skill in writing great poetry in the medium of blank verse. In all these respects Marlowe anticipated and paved the way for Shakespeare.

SECTION IV SHAKESPEARE.

1. Shakespeare's Life and Literary Career.

William Shakespeare was born in Stratford-on-Avon in 1564. His father was a trader in all kinds of agricultural products as well as many manufactured articles, including corn, wool, malt, meat, skins and leather. Later he became alderman, bailiff, and chief alderman, so that Shakespeare spent his early youth in a rather affluent bourgeois family. The boy went to the grammar school at Stratford and there he learned Latin and a little Greek, but he could not finish his schooling because his father soon got into financial difficulties. He got married to a woman several years his senior, Anne Hathaway, a yeoman's daughter. In 1585 or 1586 he left Stratford for London. According to one tradition it was because he was prosecuted by a certain big land-lord Sir Thomas Lucy for deer-stealing. Shortly after his arrival in London, he got employment either in or near a playhouse, taking care of gentlemen's horses or serving as a prompter's attendant. Then he became an actor and later started to write plays, at first possibly in collaboration with other playwrights or engaged in revising old plays. He probably began writing plays in 1588 – 1590, but at least by 1592 he had already achieved some success in playwriting which led to an attack on him by an older dramatist Robert Greene. In his pamphlet "A Groatsworth of Wit Bought with a Million of Repentances" Greene referred viciously to "the only Shake-scene in the country", "an upstart crow" who stole from other writers. In the meantime, Shake-speare's two non-dramatic poems were published, "Venus and Adonis" in 1593 and "The Rape of Lucrece" in 1594, both dedicated to his patron the Earl of Southampton. Both poems achieved popularity and were highly praised by critics at the time, and several editions were published within a few years' time. Shakespeare also wrote sonnets, both in his earlier years and after, and the total of his 154 sonnets were published without the auther's consent in 1609. Shakespeare continued to be an actor and to write plays, his dramatic career lasting for more than twenty years. Many of his plays were published during his lifetime and generally known as "quartos", though they apparently appeared without his permission or even knowledge, and then after his death, in 1623, a collection of his plays, 36 in all ("Pericles" not included), was published by two of his friends, and now known as the First Folio. In his later years Shakespeare also became a shareholder in playhouses. In 1611 or 1612 he retired or partly retired from London and bought a house in his native town Startford and went back to live there. After that he still visited London at times but did not seem to write much or pay much attention to theatrical activities in the last few years of his life. He died in Stratford in 1616.

Shakespeare's career as a dramatist may be conveniently divided into three (or four) periods. The earliest period, that of apprenticeship, dated from around 1590 (or 1588) to about 1600 (or 1601), including his earliest plays, either in collaboration with or in imitation of other playwrights, nine of his ten history plays (except "Henry VIII"), two of his well-known early tragedies ("Romeo and Juliet" and "Julius Caesar") and all his important "romantic" comedies. The second or his most important period stretched roughly from 1601 to 1608, including all his great tragedies ("Hamlet", "Othello", "King Lear", "Macbeth", etc.) and some of his earlier tragi-comedies. The third and last period dated from 1609 to 1612 or 1613, including chiefly his three last tragicomedies. Those who suggest four periods instead of three generally break the first period into two, making the year 1594 or 1595 as the line of demarcation between the period of apprenticeship and that of chiefly the great "romantic" comedies. The division of Shakespeare's plays into different periods is to help us in arriving at a better understanding of the development of his dramatic genius, though the dating of his dramas has been a very arduous task for scholars and in a number of cases cannot be accurately ascertained.

2. **Shakespeare's Poems and Sonnets.**

Just as a great number of English dramas (as many as 40) of the late 16th and early 17th centuries have been attributed to Shakespeare's authorship, so quite a few of the Elizabethan poems have been considered as possibly his also, but Shakespeare's authentic non-dramatic poetry consists only of two narrative poems "Venus and Adonis" and "The Rape of Lucrece", plus his sequence of 154 sonnets.

"Venus and Adonis" and "The Rape of Lucrece" were the two earliest of Shakespeare's works to appear in print and they brought greater fame and popularity to the poet immediately and shortly after their publication than did his early plays of the same period. However, these two poems are not unsimilar to the narrative poems by other English poets of the age and have generally been considered not much superior to most of them.   "Venus and Adonis" tells the story, based on "Metamorphosis" of the ancient Roman writer Ovid, of how Venus the Goddess of Love was in love with the handsome boy Adonis and how the latter was killed by a boar while hunting.   The poem contains some vivid pictures of the amorous Venus and the wayward Adonis and a frank eulogy of earthly love which may be regarded as a healthy anti-dote to the asceticism of the Middle Ages.   "The Rape of Lucrece", a tragic tale about the chaste Roman dame Lucrece who was raped by the terrible Tarquin, committed suicide and then was avenged, condemns lust and tyranny and praises healthful love.   In these two poems we can only see the youthful poet's skill in creating vivid scenes and colourful imageries and in employing rich, decorative language and a supple verse rhythm.

Shakespeare's sonnets were written either in a long stretch of time from 1594 – 5 up to 1609 when they were published, or chiefly in the earlier years of the poet's career, most of them between 1593 and 1596, and all before 1600.   A host of problems connected with them have led to arduous investigations and endless disputes among Shakespearean scholars and researchers. In the famous "Dedication" to these sonnets upon their first publication in 1609, the signature "T.T." has now generally been identified with Thomas Thorpe the publisher, while the "Mr. W.H." mentioned as "the only begetter" of these sonnets has been assigned to William Herbert, Earl of Pembroke, or Henry

Wriothesley, Earl of Southampton, or some one who got hold of the manuscript and gave it to Thorpe for publication. While the above controversies still remain to be settled, there are other questions raised in connection with these 154 sonnets that evolve round the subject matter in these sonnets: (1) Who were "a man right fair" and "a woman coloured ill" (or the "Dark Lady")? (2) Did Shakespeare write these sonnets purely as literary exercise because sonneteering was the fashion in his day or did he use them to reveal his innermost thoughts and feelings? What topical allusions to events of Shakespeare's age and of the poet's personal life may be traced in one or another of the sonnets in this sequence? These are interesting questions and in a sense rather essential to a full understanding and evaluation of these sonnets, but it seems well nigh impossible to arrive at any definite and reliable conclusions on any of these questions. However, at least we may safely affirm that Shakespeare in some of these sonnets did refer to a handsome friend (possibly his patron) and in some others did speak of a "dark lady" (real or imaginary; if imaginary then the poet was following the poetic convention of the day), that if the poet in some of the sonnets seemed to be merely sonneteering for fashion's sake, at least in a number of the sonnets he was expressing his genuine sentiments and thoughts, and that quite likely the poet alluded to certain contemporary events in some of his sonnets and especially to his personal life. And, above all, a careful examination of the sonnets should reveal to us some of the poet's views toward the society of his time and toward his own experience in life.

So sometimes amid his entreaties of love the poet would venture his mild criticism of the prevailing conditions at the royal court in England at the time (e.g., "monarch's plague, this flattery", in Sonnet 114; "twixt vows and change decrees of kings", in Sonnet 115; about "great princes' favourites", that "at a frown they in their glory die", in Sonnet 25), and sometimes he would condemn certain common social vices in connection with his declarations of love (e.g., against "lust" in Sonnet 129; against "slander" in Sonnet 70; against the worship of high birth or wealth and against indulgence in gay clothes or in hunting or racing, in Sonnet 91), but more frequently the poet would voice through the utterance of his own personal miseries his criticism on certain social evils (e.g., bewailing his lowly state of an actor and criticising the society's contempt for theatrical folk, in Sonnet 110; pitying himself for having been slandered by evil tongues, in Sonnets 111 and 121;weeping over his "outcast state", as in Sonnet 29, "grieve at grievances foregone", as in Sonnet 30). The most striking specimen among the whole lot is the well-known 66th sonnet which, except for its very last line, has hardly anything to do with the supposed theme of love, but is a very eloquent and comprehensive exposé of the social evils of the poet's age that must have shocked and irritated him. Not only can we find here a vivid picture of the English society as Shakespeare saw it, but the poet is obviously lodging his strong protest against many of the degenerating and corrupting phenomena of his time.

A few of the sonnets are known for the sheer haunting beauty of verse and contain lines to be ever remembered. There is the well-known 18th sonnet that begins with "Shall I compare thee to a summer's day?" There are the much quoted lines on steadfast love in the 116th sonnet:
> "Let me not to the marriage of true minds
> Admit impediments. Love is not love
> Which alters when it alteration finds."

But above all, occasionally, Shakespeare seems very definitely to have bared his soul to his readers, in such lines as: "Desiring this man's art and that man's scope" (Sonnet 29), "And heavily from woe to woe tell o'er/The sad account of fore-bemoaned moan" (Sonnet 30), "No longer mourn for me when I am dead" (Sonnet 71), and
> "Alas, 'tis true I have gone here and there
> And made myself a motley to the view,
> Gored mine own thoughts, sold cheap what is most dear,
> Made old offences of affections new;" (Sonnet 110)

These few lines are comparable to the best passages in Shakespeare's great comedies and tragedies.

Regarding the literary form of these sonnets, it should be mentioned that the language Shakespeare employs in most of these sonnets has the distinction over that of most other sonneteers of his age in its great economy and intensity, and that the poet makes supple and adroit use of the English or Shakespearan sonnet form (though it was actually first used by Surrey). Both in theme and in literary form Shakespeare's sonnets as a sequence are superior to those of the other poets of Elizabethan England.

3. **Early Period of Shakespeare's Plays: History Plays ("Richard III", "Henry IV", Parts 1 and 2, "Henry V"); Early Tragedies ("Romeo and Juliet", "Julius Caesar"); Comedies ("The Merchant of Venice", "Much Ado about Nothing", "As You Like It", "Twelfth Night").**

The first or the early period of Shakespeare's drama includes nine out of ten History Plays (except "Henry VIII"), three tragedies ("Titus Andronicus", "Remeo and Juliet" and "Julius Caesar"), experimental comedies of early apprenticeship ("Love's Labour's Lost", "The Two Gentlemen of Verona" and "The Comedy of Errors"), comedies of the fantastic or farcical type ("A Midsummer Night's Dream", "The Taming of the Shrew" and "The Merry Wives of Windsor") and mature, "romantic" comedies ("The Merchant of Venice", "Much Ado about Nothing", "As You Like It" and "Twelfth Night").

Of the nine history plays of the early period, the three parts of "Henry VI" are unquestionably the earliest and also the first plays to have brought fame to Shakespeare, but they also involve a question of authorship, for most scholars agreed that not everything in all the three plays was from Shakespeare's pen and that his share was larger in Part III than in Part II while that in Part I was negligible. As to who were Shakespeare's collaborators opinions differ, with Marlowe as the likeliest to have had a fair share while almost all the other University Wits with the exception of Lyly (i.e., Kyd, Peele, Greene, Lodge and Nashe) could have had a hand, more or less, in this or that of the three history plays. The First Part of "Henry VI" is undoubtedly the least important of the three: the only thing worthy of note is the poet's spirit of patriotism as he created a general atmosphere of mourning over the loss of English territories in France as a result of civil contention among the barons and lords under a weak child king. Part II is more significant. Here we have striking scenes of class struggle between the oppressors and the oppressed or more specifically between the peasants and plebeians on the one hand and the landed aristocrats and city noblemen on the other. However, Shakespeare did not seem to approve of Jack Cade's rising of 1450 but rather ridiculed the popular leader as an ignorant impostor, though certain ideals of the peasants' risings of those days, like the lowering of the price of bread and the proclamation that "all things shall be common", were apparently welcomed. Besides, in the first act of this play, there appeared one peasant in a petition against a landlord for robbing him of his house and lands and wife and another petitioning against the Duke of Suffolk for enclosing the commons of Melford (Act I, Scene 3). Then, in the second act, with there was a case of a single combat between an apprentice and his master, the former triumphing over the latter and other apprentices standing by and cheering the victor (Act II, Scene 3). In these three cases Shakespeare showed his unmistakable sympathy for the oppressed against the oppressors. This play has the further merit of condemning the terrible War of the Roses between the feudal barons, mourning the pitiful downfall of the weak but upright figure of Humphrey the Duke of Gloucester and showing gratification over the deserved exile and death of the shameful Duke of Suffolk. The Second Part of "Henry VI" is nevertheless a very immature play artistically. In the Third Part of "Henry VI" the terrible ravages of the War of the Roses were highlighted by the scene of a son mistakenly killing his father and of a father equally mistakenly killing his son during the confusion of enlistment and of battle (Act II, Scene 5), while the treachery and faithlessness of the noblemen who would join one side one moment and turn to the other side the next as well as the ruthless bloodshed and villainy of Gloucester were vividly presented and sharply censured by the dramatist. The soliloquies of Gloucester (later Richard III), well-known on the English stage, marked the effective use for the first time of long soliloquizing for central figures in Shakespearan tragedies.

"Richard III", the last play of Shakespeare's first tetralogy of historical drama that included the three parts of "Henry VI", tells the story of Richard the Duke of Gloucester's ambitions and his steps taken to seize the throne, then his success and accession as Richard III and finally his downfall and death. With the repeated use of soliloquy that reveals Richard's innermost thoughts of villainy and his schemes for winning the crown, the scenes unfold themselves one after another: his tricks to imprison and then to murder his brother Clarence, his dramatic and successful wooing of Anne the widow of Henry VI's son he has murdered, his schemes to arrest and then kill the faithful supporters of his brother Edward IV after the latter's death, his machination to make the mayor of London come with some citizens to ask him to be king, and then his accession to the throne and the murder of his nephew the young king Edward V. Then, almost immediately after that, Buckingham who has ever helped Richard to attain kingship rebels and is crushed, but Richmond (the future Henry VII) comes with an army from France and Richard is defeated and killed at the battle of Bosworth (in 1485). This play was obviously written under the influence of the Senecan tragedies of blood and revenge but more directly under that of Marlowe's "one-man tragedy" which in its turn was based on the medieval concept of tragedy about the hero's rise to success and then his downfall. But the character Richard III is here most vividly drawn as an archvillain or a typical representative of Machiavellianism, and the obvious condemnation of such a figure as well as the exposé of brutal bloodshed and unscrupulous treachery and intrigue among the princes and the courtiers during the War of the Roses quite definitely serve to show the poet's fears of a possible civil war breaking out and his denunciation of intrigue and treachery at the court of Queen Elizabeth. "Richard III" in this sense is a continuation of the three parts of "Henry VI", but as a play it has much greater dramatic power and artistic unity and is the first important history play (or tragedy) by Shakespeare.

"King John" is comparatively unimportant among Shakespeare's history plays, though it contains the brilliant portrayal of Faulconbridge the Bastard, as a typical Renaissance figure who detects in the new human relations in the rising capitalist world the dominant element of "Commodity" which may be interpreted as "self-interest" or "profit" (or even "cash nexus").

"Richard II" has been associated by Shakespearean scholars historically with the agitation for the revolt of Lord Essex against Queen Elizabeth and literarily with Marlowe's "Edward the Second". Actually it contains a condemnation by Shakespeare simultaneously of two types of kings, the king who believes in the divine right of kings, levies heavy taxes upon the people and acts with absolute power against the feudal barons, as represented by Richard II, and the king who employs tricks to curry favour with the common people and to seize royal power by unscrupulous means, as represented by Bolingbroke who became Henry IV. Only this twofold condemnation can explain the surprising change of Richard II from the hateful tyrant at the beginning of the play to the pitiful figure of a sad mourner of his own fate after the third act, and only this can account for the equally surprising change of Bolingbroke from an apparently admirable person in the first act to the hypocrite-turned-tyrant-plus-murderer after he succeeds in seizing power in Act III.

The two parts of "Henry IV" and "Henry V", coming at the end of the series of Shakespeare's nine history plays, constitute the highwater mark of the poet's achievement in this dramatic genre. "Henry IV", Parts I and II censured sharply the ambitions of the feudal barons in England that led to civil wars and political instability while "Henry V" eulogized an "ideal" monarch who worked for the welfare of the whole nation. Such an attitude of Shakespeare's in the three plays coincided with the interests of the rising bourgeoisie at the time and so has its progressive significance.

The king in "Henry V" is one of the few great heroes in Shakespeare's plays. Especially in the scene of Henry V's inspection of the camp and in his soliloquy on the eve of the famous battle of Agincourt, we find Shakespeare the poet of the rising bourgeoisie declaiming the bourgeois theory of democracy and social equality. "The King is but a man, as I am", may be a remark containing irony because the words come from the very lips of the king in disguise, but the speech is nevertheless an unmistakable slogan suggesting liberty and democracy. After all, the English bourgeois revolution was less than half a century away.

In the two parts of "Henry IV" we have the inimitable figure of Falstaff who may be only the principal character of the sub-plot in the two plays but whose vivid portrayal has earned for him an enviable place in the history of English literature.

Sir John Falstaff was a feudal knight, who, living at an age when feudalism was declining and yielding its place to the new bourgeois society, adopted many of the new bourgeois ways while retaining certain old feudal practices and sentiments. He was old and fat and deprived of his former feudal means of livelihood but he indulged in wine, women and song and tried every means to obtain the almighty cash with which to satiate his carnal pleasures in life. So he mixed on the one hand with the young prince Hal and on the other with a group of dissolute companions and prostitutes and bawds and tavern-keepers, and in order to obtain enough money for his huge expenses resorted even to robbing on the highway, to taking bribes while recruiting soldiers, to cheating poor tavern hostesses and to imposing on ignorant country justices by boasts and false promises. He was thoroughly despicable, particularly because he was cunning and eloquent, able to defend himself self-righteously or shamefacedly against other people's accusations, and when he was finally cornered and his clever arguments were no longer of any avail to him he laughed away his follies or his cowardice with cynical remarks. So he became an extremely typical figure of the degenerating feudal nobility finding his way about in the new bourgeois environment in a big city, and he was comical rather than pathetic because he did not take his defeats in life lying down but acted knave-like to grab all he could while pretending to be honourable and respectable. He is one of the most successful character-portraits in the whole Shakespearean gallery, and is indeed a "typical character in typical circumstances". Falstaff again appears in "The Merry Wives of Windsor", but shown there as a sort of charlatan making love to a pair of respectable women of the city bourgeoisie he is no longer the brilliant figure that he is in the two parts of "Henry IV", but seems to be simply a ridiculous person to be laughed at, without the gift of wit to justify himself with cynical remarks or return laughter for laughter.

The earliest of Shakespeare's tragedies, "Titus Andronicus", based on ancient Roman history, is a crude Senecan melodrama of vengeance and sudden death, and whether or not Shakespeare had any share in it, it is certainly a very immature work of the young dramatist.

"Romeo and Juliet" is one of Shakespeare's best known tragedies and it fully deserves its fame though it was the product of a youthful poet, judged both from its theme and from its artistic form. Romeo and Juliet belong to two families engaged in family feud of long standing, but the two fall in love and are secretly married. When Romeo is banished for killing one of Juliet's kinsmen Tybalt and the girl's parents insist on marrying her to another, the friar who has married the two lovers tries to help them, but his plan fails owing to several unhappy accidents, and the young lovers die one after the other. In this tradegy Shakespeare attacks the feudal world of family feud by placing in it two young lovers with humanist ideals of love and then working out their inevitable tragedy in the hostile environment. Though the incidents in the drama seem to suggest that the tragedy is due more to accidents than to the social contradictions because if some of the friar's plans hadn't gone awry the lovers could still have a chance to gain their eventual happiness, yet to think that way would be to overlook the irreconcilable conflict between the terrible feudal bondage of family feud and the young lovers' daring yet inexperienced attempts to shatter that bondage, for such a contradiction must necessarily lead to tragedy earlier or later, in one way or in another. And the tragedy was rendered with such power and beauty via the enormously successful character-portraits of the hero and the heroine, so successful that the name of Romeo has since been identified with the acme of a dashing young lover and Juliet has become a synonym for an ill-starred heroine of great beauty, strong will and true passion. Their youthful love is told with fervid lyricism by the youthful poet in brilliant dialogue and elegant verse, highlighted in the famous balcony scene (Act II, Scene 2) and the poignant parting scene (Act III, Scene 5) which have ever been remembered as two of the truly great love scenes in all literature. However, the numerous mishaps befalling the lovers one after another are fatal blows to the plot construction and the lavish, ornamental language employed often produces a cloying effect upon the reader. One cannot fail to detect in this tragedy the limitations of a young poet not yet possessed of the sureness of touch which was to be his in the great tragedies of a later period.

"Julius Caesar" is the second of Shakespeare's tragedies based on ancient Roman history, with North's translation of Plutarch's "Lives" as source material. The Roman conspirators led by Brutus and Cassius assassinated Julius Caesar presumably to check the latter's dictatorial ambitions, and then the civil war broke out between the conspirators and Caesar's friends Antony and Octavius, ending in the defeat and death of Brutus and Cassius. The real hero in the play is not Ceasar but Brutus who ranks high among the great humanist heroes in Shakespeare's plays because he is represented as a man of high democratic ideals working selflessly in the interests of the people against enemies of freedom. In this sense this play may well be considered the harbinger of the great tragedies of Shakespeare's period of maturity when he portrayed vividly men with high ideals coming into conflict with the ugly social realities of the feudal-bourgeois world and when he delved deeply into the inner workings of the minds of his tragic heroes. Of course there are some serious flaws in the character-portrayal of Brutus whose motivation for the assassination of Caesar seems at times to be a dubious case of self-interest versus true selfless idealism. However, the two speeches delivered after Caesar's death, one by Brutus and the other by Antony, are certainly well known specimens of great oration and great prose.

The three experimental comedies of early apprenticeship ("Love's Labour's Lost", "The Comedy of Errors" and "The Two Gentlemen of Verona") are ineffective attempts of the yet inexperienced and imitative dramatist. The first falls frankly under the influence of Lyly and his euphuism and the second is almost an adaptation of Plautus' "Menaechmi" and "Amphitruo", while the third follows rather closely the tradition of the romantic comedies of Greene and Peele and Lyly and serves as a preliminary exercise in preparation for the more mature comedies like "As You Like It" and "Twelfth Night". These three were followed by another group of three comedies: one fantasy and two farces, "A Midsummer Night's Dream", "The Taming of the Shrew" and "The Merry Wives of Windsor". The last of the group, according to one tradition, is supposed to have been written by the poet when Queen Elizabeth wanted to see the fat old knight in love after she had enjoyed the character of Falstaff in the two parts of "Henry IV". Whether this is true or not is of little importance, but the play is far inferior to "Henry IV", and Falstaff in this later drama no longer has the inimitable humour and witty cynicism that made him so fascinating as the pal of the young prince and the resourceful participant in numerous comic incidents. Whether Shakespeare wrote the whole of "The Taming of the Shrew" has been a problem to Shakespearean scholars, but the play was obviously partly adapted from an older play "The Taming of a Shrew". The Petruchio-Katharina scenes which constitute the major plot are certainly a tour de force that contains much effective dialogue and some adept character-portrayal, though the situations are too farcical to be realistic, and the theme of taming shrews belongs rather to the old feudal than to the bourgeois society. "A Midsummer Night's Dream" is a play of fantasy, with the fairyland background of Titania and Oberon and Puck, but it is also a farce, with the plot around the lovers hinging upon the love juice, and the subplot of a play within the play is simply slapstick comedy to satirize some of the clumsy and pointless dramas of the poet's contemporaries.

Of Shakespeare's four mature, "romantic" comedies, "The Merchant of Venice" is certainly the most outstanding, though the earliest in its date of composition. It is essentially different from the three others in its much more serious theme which reveals clearly Shakespeare's ever-present, strong sympathy for the oppressed, and his almost instinctive antipathy against oppression of any kind, sometimes quite in spite of himself. Bassanio, a poor Venetian gentleman, asks his rich friend Antonio, the "merchant of Venice", for a loan of three thousand ducats in order to go and court Portia, a rich heiress of Belmont, but Antonio whose wealth is all invested in merchandise and ships for foreign trade has no ready cash and so he asks Shylock, a Jewish usurer, for a loan. Shylock has been ill-treated by Antonio and other Venetian gentlemen because he is a Jew, so he now consents to the loan on condition that Antonio sign a bond agreeing to the forfeit of a pound of his flesh if the money is not returned on the appointed day. Bassanio wins Portia, but Antonio failing to repay Shylock is threatened with the loss of a pound of his flesh which naturally means the loss of his life. All efforts to persuade Shylock to forego the bond by accepting many times the money loaned are in vain, when Portia disguising herself as a young doctor of laws defeats Shylock at the court by ordering him to cut exactly one pound of Antonio's flesh, no more and no less, and to shed not a single drop of blood, with the threat of heavy punishment by law if otherwise. Shylock beats a retreat and asks now only to be repaid the loan, but he is further charged with the crime of an alien conspiring against the life of a Venetian. The Duke of Venice foregoes the death sentence but decrees taking away from Shylock all his wealth, half of it to be given to the state and half to Antonio. Antonio gives up his half by asking Shylock to turn Christian and to will the money to his daughter Jessica who has run away with her Christian husband Lorenzo.

The central theme of the play is obviously the triumph of love (between Portia and Bassanio) and friendship (between Antonio and Bassanio) over insatiable greed and brutality (as represented by Shylock), and there can hardly be any question that Shakespeare meant to exalt the ingenious heroine Portia and the two great friends (Antonio and Bassanio) whom she eventually saves from the barbarous clutches of the villain (Shylock) and that a completely happy ending is brought about when the villain is punished, the merchant's ships all come home and the three pairs of lovers live happily ever after. Of course, as minor issues, Lorenzo's inheritance of half of Shylock's property and Jessica's turning Christian are obviously also intended as events calling for joy and celebration. And such a conclusion was the most natural thing in the world for the playwright as well as for his Elizabethan audience, when anti-semitic sentiments had risen to a high pitch in London following the trial and execution of Queen Elizabeth's Jewish physician Dr. Lopez on a charge of treason and Christopher Marlowe had just written his topical play "The Jew of Malta". Yet even in such an environment and at such a moment, in Shylock's vociferous complaints of his terrible sufferings resulting from racial discrimination and religious persecution ("The Merchant of Venice", Act I, Scene 3, lines 108 – 130 and Act III, Scene 1), we can hear quite unmistakably Shakespeare's own voice speaking on the Jew's behalf, and with great vehemence sympathizing with the oppressed Shylock while condemning racial persecution in general, as if the poet had clean forgotten his original intentions of censuring the Jew as a usurer and cruel extortioner deserving the severest punishment. That Shakespeare should sometimes condemn Shylock and sometimes sympathize with him has led to much confusion for Shakespearean scholars and critics and the general reading public, to the extent that the play has been regarded by some as not a pure comedy but a tragi-comedy, and some distinguished Shakespearean actors in the 19th century (e.g., Edmund Kean) even played the part of Shylock as a tragic role. The solution to this dilemma in our interpretation of this play can only be gained if we think of Shakespeare as ever on the side of the oppressed no matter who it was: When Shylock accuses Antonio of persecuting him, the poet sympathized with the Jew, but when the-oppressed-turned-oppressor persists in killing the merchant, the playwright sympathized with Antonio. Here we see the true progressive significance of "The Merchant of Venice" and of its author: consistent hatred for the oppressors and sympathy for the oppressed.

Two other things must be mentioned in connection with "The Merchant of Venice": the heroine Portia and the use of disguise as a dramatic device. Portia is a great character-portrait and the earliest of the series of great heroines in Shakespeare's comedies. Like Rosalind in "As You Like It", Beatrice in "Much Ado about Nothing" and Viola in "Twelfth Night", Portia in "The Merchant of Venice" is a new woman of the Renaissance, active, vivacious, capable, clever and serious-minded, who not only frees herself from the usual feudal fetters for women but even outshines many men in many ways, including her lover and husband Bassanio. The device of women disguised as men (Portia and her maid Nerissa), in the famous court scene and in the subsequent scenes dealing with the rings, are not only full of fun and dramatic excitement but also contributive to the portrayal of character. This dramatic device of disguise, borrowed from Greene and first employed by Shakespeare in "The Two Gentlemen of Verona", is used most effectively here as also in "As You Like It" and "Twelfth Night" and in a tragicomedy of the dramatist's last period, "Cymbeline".

"Much Ado about Nothing" contains a dual plot, one about the lovely Hero whose love affair with Claudio almost ends in tragedy as a result of the trickeries of a minor villain Don John, and the other about Beatrice and Benedick who fall in love with each other partly with the help of their affectionate but scheming friends. There are several effective comic scenes of dramatic irony when the two major characters Benedick and Beatrice are tricked into believing that the loved one is dying of love for him or her but is too proud to declare it openly to the beloved. Also a new woman of the Renaissance breaking through the feudal fetters of the Middle Ages, Beatrice distinguishes herself as the most witty and eloquent heroine in Shakespeare's comedies, and is well matched with Benedick, the only hero in Shakespeare's comedies whose wit and general capabilities can fully rival with and are not eclipsed by those of the brilliant heroine he loves. This pair of lovers, with their scintillating dialogue and brilliant soliloquies which show Shakespeare's light and elegant prose at its best, suggest their complete liberation from the age-old shackles of asceticism and inequality between the sexes. In their speeches we find Shakespeare making the best use of the popular euphuistic style for his dramatic purpose of witty dialogue and meditative soliloquy. In "Much Ado about Nothing" the figure of Dogberry as the ignorant and malaprop constable is one of the outstanding clowns in Shakespeare's comedies.

"As You Like It", with its story adapted from Thomas Lodge's prose romance "Rosalynde", is a pastoral play based on the literary tradition of the idealization of country life, an age-old tradition which had its origin in Hellenistic Greek literature (Theocritus) and ancient Roman poetry (Vergil).

Duke Senior's younger brother Frederick usurps the throne and drives away not only the rightful duke, but also his niece Rosalind, while a courtier Oliver maltreats his youngest brother Orlando and drives him out of his home. Rosalind and Orlando, after falling in love at first sight, both eventually arrive in the Forest of Arden where Duke Senior lives in exile. Rosalind's disguise as a man leads to many comic scenes after she meets Orlando, and the play ends in perfect happiness when Duke Frederick repents and returns the dukedom to Duke Senior, Oliver and Orlando are reconciled, and Rosalind and Orlando finally are happily married, together with three other pairs of lovers. The Forest of Arden, where the exiled duke lives happily with a group of his former courtiers and where later his daughter Rosalind and his niece Celia as well as Orlando and Oliver also resort, is the background of the drama and is idealized as a land happy and free from cares and there are many delightful songs celebrated for their spontaneity and lyricism ("Under the Greenwood Tree", "Blow, blow, thou winter wind" and "It was a lover and his lass"). Here we have the brilliant portrayal of the heroine Rosalind, the great clown Touchstone, and the melancholy philosophical Jacques, and also the effective use of the dramatic device of a woman disguised as a man. Jacques' lengthy speech of "All the world's a stage/And all the men and women merely players" is a true gem of Shakespeare the actor-playwright's carefully meditated comment on life, couched in inimitable blank verse.

"Twelfth Night, or What You Will", the last of the series of Shakespeare's four romantic love comedies, evolves round the love of the duke for Olivia, of Olivia for Viola (in her disguise as a man) and of

Viola for the duke. Numerous comic scenes result from Viola's disguise, and then dénouement comes when Viola's twin brother Sebastian appears and marries Olivia, making it necessary (and expedient) for Viola to shed her disguise and marry the duke. However, the highlights in "Twelfth Night" are not so much the theme of love involving Viola and Duke Orsino and Olivia or the character-portrayal of the vivacious heroine Viola or the use of the dramatic device of a woman disguised as a man and the consequent dramatic irony arising out of mistaken identity, but the most engrossing episodes in the comedy have to do with Olivia's steward Malvolio and with the tricks played upon him by Olivia's maid Maria and the others. The overmuch indulgence in carnal pleasures as practised by Olivia's uncle Sir Toby and his friend Sir Andrew is somewhat connived at by the author while the central butt of satire is rather the asceticism practised by Malvolio as a Puritan. In an age in which the terrific struggle between Puritanism and the Cavalier sentiments of many aristocrats and courtiers grew more and more intense and in which the theatres were considered as immoral and plays could not be produced within the immediate city limits of London, it is not to be wondered at that Shakespeare as an actor and playwright and shareholder of playhouses should subject Malvolio the Puritan to open ridicule. Sir Toby's brilliant remark: "Dost thou think, because thou art virtuous, there shall be no more cakes and ale?" and Feste's song: "What's love? 'Tis not hereafter" fully illustrate Shakespeare's youthful spirit of jollity and joie de vivre at its height, and indicate the poet's approval of the Renaissance attitude of enjoying present life and present mirth in opposition to the medieval emphasis on future life and otherworldliness.

4. **Mature Period of Shakespeare's Plays: Tragedies ("Hamlet", "Othello","King Lear","Macbeth","Antony and Cleopatra","Coriolanus", "Timon of Athens"); Tragi-Comedies ("Measure for Measure", "All's Well that Ends Well", "Troilus and Cressida").**
   The second or mature period of Shakespeare's dramatic career includes the poet's great tragedies (beginning with "Hamlet", through

"Othello", "King Lear", "Macbeth", "Antony and Cleopatra" and "Coriolanus" to "Timon of Athens") and his earlier tragi-comedies ("Troilus and Cressida", "All's Well that Ends Well" and "Measure for Measure"). These plays were quite different from those of the poet's early period, not only because he had grown more mature but also because the English society had undergone much fundamental change in the transition from Elizabethan England in the last decades of the 16th century to the new regime of James I in the early years of the 17th century. Shakespeare's great tragedies and his "dark" tragicomedies, written in the very first decade of the 17th century, naturally reflect that age of social and political unrest rather than the poet's own life of "tragic gloom" as suggested by some critics. And this faithful reflection of the social reality of the time was claimed, as it were, by the poet himself through the mouth of Hamlet, that the "end" or purpose of drama "was and is, to hold, as it were, the mirror up to nature: to show virtue her own feature, scorn her own image, and the very age and body of the time his form and pressure." At that time, the co-operation between the monarch (the feudal ruler) and the parliament (or the bourgeoisie) which had worked quite nicely in the late 16th century was becoming more and more strained, especially after the accession of James I who believed in the divine right of kings whereas the bourgeoisie wanted more and still more freedom with their greater accumulation of wealth and expansion of trade. Also, the luxury of James I and the dissolute living of the cavaliers led to further moral degeneracy among the aristocrats which also spread to the townspeople, and with the development of capitalism, there were more greed and selfishness and hypocrisy and treachery among the bourgeoisie as well as among the courtiers. So, even in the tragi-comedies of the dramatist's second period, terrible crimes were committed everywhere and dark fate seemed to hover over all the characters, and even the happy endings in these plays were not convincing nor really happy. In the great tragedies, the sharpened contradictions in the political and social arena are reflected through the life-and-death struggles between the evil forces (Claudius in "Hamlet", Iago in "Othello", Goneril and Regan and Edmund in "Lear",

etc.) and the idealist heroes or heroines (Hamlet, Othello and Desdemona, Cordelia, etc.), with the latter all becoming victims in their conflict with tyranny and hypocrisy and treachery, but those victims are
shown by Shakespeare to be morally victorious in the end because the
poet cherished the illusion of the so-called "poetic justice", believing
that villains may triumph for a time but not for long while the righteous
ones may die but will eventually earn their deserved after-fame.

"Hamlet", written in 1601 – 2, was the first of the great tragedies.
The chief elements in the play: the story of murder and revenge,
the appearance of a ghost, the performance of a play within a play, the
madness both real and pretended of the central characters — all these
were nothing new with Shakespeare, they had all appeared in an earlier
play "The Spanish Tragedy" by Thomas Kyd, if not in another earlier
Hamlet play probably also by Kyd (known as "Ur-Hamlet"). And
the story of Hamlet the Prince of Denmark had its source in a book of
Danish history by Saxo Grammaticus. But Shakespeare took the
story and all the other suggestions and wrote a play which reflected
his age and his own innermost thoughts and feelings.

The story in Shakespeare's play is none too complicated. Hamlet,
the central character, is told by his father's ghost that the latter has been
murdered by Hamlet's uncle Claudius who is now ruling as king and
has married the former queen, Hamlet's mother. Hamlet pretends to
be mad while planning for revenge and at the same time trying to make
sure about his uncle's guilt. A group of actors arrive and Hamlet asks
them to stage a play of murder before the king, and the latter, conscience-
stricken, leaves the performance before it is through. Hamlet is now
sure of his uncle's crime and decides to kill the culprit, but he desists as
he passes by the king's chamber and sees the villain praying. Hamlet
then goes to his mother's room and there he kills an important courtier
Polonius, mistaking him for his uncle. For this slaughter Hamlet is
sent to England by his uncle, to be beheaded there upon arrival. But
Hamlet escapes and comes home, and he meets Polonius' son Laertes
in a fencing match as arranged by his uncle. Treachery does its work
but the villain also goes to his deserved punishment and death, and all

the principal characters die in the final scene.

Hamlet is one of the several idealists (or Renaissance humanists as some critics would have it) created by Shakespeare as an embodiment of the poet's own ideals. In his case, first and foremost is his personal ideal, that of filial piety and a strong sense of justice that demands revenge. But he has his social and political ideals too. On the one hand he envisages the infinite capabilities of man: "What a piece of work is man; how noble in reason! how infinite in faculty! in form and moving how express and admirable! in action how like an angel! in apprehension how like a god! the beauty of the world! the paragon of animals!" On the other hand he sees and hopes to eliminate the innumerable social evils besetting and enfettering human beings, as he speaks of "the slings and arrows of outrageous fortune" and "a sea of troubles" and

> "the whips and scorns of time,
> The oppressor's wrong, the proud man's contumely,
> The pangs of despised love, the law's delay,
> The insolence of office and the spurns
> The patient merit of the unworthy takes."

So Hamlet engages himself first of all in personal revenge but at the same time attempts in a rather vague way to set right the "time" that is "out of joint". He is an idealist of a sort but his chief objective is personal revenge, and only secondarily does he also think of eliminating the social evils of the day, and so the extremely high tribute paid to the hero and to the play by certain critics — the eulogy of Hamlet as a great humanist aiming at social reforms on an extensive scale and of "Hamlet" as a great tragedy of a great humanist hero — is quite obviously over-praise. However, from the artistic point of view, the excellent portrayal of the hero's character and the superb blank verse employed certainly place the play among the three or four truly great tragedies of the great poet. Hamlet's actions and speeches toward the numerous other characters in the play, toward Claudius and Polonius and Queen Gertrude and Ophelia, toward Horatio and Rosencrantz and Guildenstern and Osric, toward Laertes and the gravediggers and the players, show the prince to be a man of infinite variety, and the charm of this manysided character of the hero is further enhanced by his numerous soliloquies, some of great length on different occasions. These soliloquies, together with all his speeches and asides, are wonderful analytical studies of the inner workings of Hamlet's mind, and such intense psychological study of the hero as a dramatic device was not introduced into European literature till the late 19th century and in some ways is not unsimilar even to the "psycho-analytical" fiction and drama of the 20th century. In this light, the comments of certain Western critics on Hamlet's indecision and delay in carrying out revenge are somewhat far-fetched and rather testify to their failure to appreciate Shakespeare's "modernity" in his attempt to delve into the psychological depth of his central character instead of merely presenting the latter's actions and words as was the general practice of his contemporary dramatists. And the scenes of the pretended madness of Hamlet and the real madness of Ophelia are well-managed and interesting, as documents of a comparative study of a psychopath and a specimen of assumed insanity. The playwright seems to have left the question unanswered as to which is the more tragic case, real madness or "madness in craft". The character-portrayal of Ophelia is in a way another master-stroke of Shakespeare's, for the gradual development in the career of this timid, naive girl, from her early conviction in Hamlet's love for her, through his later strange behaviour toward her and his unquestioned responsibility for her father's death till her singing of mad songs and finally her tragic death in the stream, is extremely well worked out, and the numerous episodes in which she makes her appearances add up to a rounded portrait of the heroine who is made up of real flesh and blood.

Of other brilliant character-portraits in "Hamlet", mention should be made particularly of King Claudius as the consummate villain who is nevertheless occasionally conscience-stricken and Polonius, a garrulous old man and a fool of a fawning courtier, both of whom deserve to have their proper places in the Shakespearean gallery of well-drawn characters.

King Claudius does not dare to punish Hamlet inside Denmark because of the latter's popularity with the people. Laertes comes with a crowd of common people to ask the king for his father's revenge, and that frightens both the queen and the king. Both incidents show the important role the common people can play in the affairs of the state, and this reflects the power of the London citizens in English history in enthroning and deposing kings (as also may be seen in Shakespeare's history plays). However, both here and in similar scenes of Roman citizens in "Julius Caesar" and "Coriolanus", as well as in certain episodes in the history plays, Shakespeare seems to have shown quite definitely his contempt for the common people as ignorant and fickle "rabble" in spite of the great potential power in politics that they possessed. The use of the ghost as the crux in the plot is inevitable because it is an integral part of the source-story, but for stage effect at times Shakespeare tries to make the ghost's appearance seem real, as in Act I, Scene 1, when the dramatist's superb manipulation even makes the scholar-skeptic Horatio "tremble and look pale" and admit that it is "something more than fantasy." But then superstition was common and prevalent in Shakespeare's day, and so we cannot blame the poet for not being an exception.

Othello, a dark-faced Moor, serves as a capable general in Venice and wins the love of a beautiful, strong-minded girl Desdemona, daughter of a senator. Her father objects to her secret marriage with the Moor, but Othello is just then much needed as commander to lead troops to a war with the Turks, and so the senator's protest is overruled by the duke and Othello goes to war on the island of Cyprus, accompanied by his new bride. After their arrival there, the Turks have already met with destruction in a sea storm and the war is over, but one of the officers under Othello, the villain Iago, hates the general for placing another man Cassio above him as lieutenant and therefore tries to destroy the Moor's happiness by convincing him of Desdemona's illicit relations with Cassio. Othello falls into the trap, kills Desdemona, and finds out the truth at last and kills himself. Iago's villainy is exposed and he is shipped back to Venice to await fit punishment.

Othello and Desdemona both rank high among the idealized figures in Shakespearean drama. They are two great lovers who love and marry each other in defiance of the seemingly insuperable racial barriers. Her father loved Othello and often invited him, but as soon as he heard of the Moor marrying his daughter, he went hurriedly to see the duke, even at the dead of night, in order to have the marriage annulled and the culprit punished.

For a moment the question of racial discrimination comes to the fore and Shakespeare obviously has his sympathy for the lovers as against the girl's father's racial prejudice. However, the main theme of the tragedy is not racial prejudice, but rather the struggle of an upright man and a pure woman with a treacherous villain and his Machiavellian tricks. Iago, whose Italian name identifies him somehow with Machiavelli, and who proves to be too much for the noble Moor, is one of the blackest villains in Shakespeare's plays and one of the most carefully drawn Shakespearean character-portraits. His words and actions that bring about tragedy, including his soliloquies, are masterfully worked out by the poet for the condemnation of Machiavellianism in the age of rising capitalism.

More than Desdemona Othello is a Renaissance humanist, an idealist whose ideals of steadfast love cannot easily be shattered. So the play is a detailed account of how Othello proceeds from his implicit faith in Desdemona's "honesty", through his first suspicions of her infidelity, to his conviction of her falseness and his final decision to smother her. From the great scene in the play, Act III, Scene 3, to the final death scene in Act V, Shakespeare gives us a most remarkable psychological study of the great general as Iago's seemingly incidental remarks of high poison and his tricks of the handkerchief gradually though almost imperceptibly set to work and the gullible lover falls step by step into the trap. And this superfine character portraiture provides us with a convincing picture of two great lovers with their true ideals doomed to tragedy when they come into grips with the ugly social realities of the day, in particular with an arch-villain of Machiavellianism among the rising bourgeoisie. The issue of racial discrimination